Legendary
Woman

Michelle McClain-Walters

CHARISMA
HOUSE

Visit the author's website at www.michellemcclainwalters.com,
MichelleMcClainBooks.com.

Cataloging-in-Publication Data is on file with the Library of Congress.
International Standard Book Number: 978-1-62999-884-8
E-book ISBN: 978-1-62999-885-5

21 22 23 24 25 — 9 8 7 6 5 4 3 2 1
Printed in the United States of America

CONTENTS

PART II:
WALKING IN THE FULLNESS OF GOD'S DESIGN

YOU WERE MADE TO BE LEGENDARY

T HROUGHOUT HISTORY, WHENEVER the fullness of time had come and it seemed the spiritual tension could increase no more, the state of the culture could be no more unsettling, and the cause of justice and righteousness was faltering, a legendary woman has arisen and stepped into her God-given place. She may have been a queen, an aviator, a businesswoman, a single mother, a political leader, an executive assistant, an educator, a scientist, a high school dropout, a health-care worker, a missionary, or a rebel. Women of all personality types, from shy and reserved to bold and courageous, and from all walks of life have stepped up and stepped out to fulfill the call of God on their lives. Ordinary women became extraordinary, became legendary, just by being willing vessels for the One who created them for a purpose.

The age we are living in is no different. In fact this is the finest hour in human history to be alive and to be a woman. The Lord Most High is activating an army of women who will lead, preach, pray, prophesy, invent, and prosper under the active guidance of the Holy Ghost. And in the midst of this activation, right before our very eyes, God is revealing His redemptive plan for women in His kingdom and restoring His original intent for the roles women are to play. Like no other time in the history of the world, women are breaking through centuries-old barriers in politics, medicine, and the workplace. Great strides have been made for gender equality, but to put it in my South Side Chicago vernacular, "You ain't seen nothin' yet!"

Something incredible is happening! Something supernatural is happening. The Lord is giving the word, and great is the company of kingdom women who will proclaim it (Ps. 68:11). They will conceive and bring forth His plans and purposes, as Sarah did. They will be silent spiritual assassins, as Jael was. They will have boldness and courage to go to war for what is right, as Joan of Arc did. They will have fierce love and driving compassion to care for "the least of these," as Mother Teresa did. They will be the next financiers that forward the Great Commission, as Lydia, Mary Magdalene, Joanna, and Susanna were (Luke 8:2–3; Acts 16:14–15). They will set out on godly quests for equality, justice, and fairness, as the daughters of Zelophehad and Rosa Parks did.

And you, beloved woman of God, are called to play a leading role. In fact I believe that is why you picked up this book, because you were made to be legendary. The providential hand of God has divinely orchestrated the events of your life to get you here, to this very moment in history in which you are coming face to face with destiny. You were made to be legendary. As you engage with the stories of legendary women in this book, you will begin to connect the dots of your own life, tracing through your past, whether scandalous or uneventful. You will see that not one tear, not one hurt, not one moment of being overlooked has been wasted. God is ready to use it all.

God's Word promises that "all things work together for good to those who love God, to those who are the called according to His purpose" (Rom. 8:28). He will work it all—the pain, the joy, and everything in between—together for good because you, woman of God, have been called according to His purpose.

Every legendary woman has to face herself and ask, "God, why do You have me here?" The answer comes when you allow the Spirit of God to lead you to the defining moment when your destiny intersects with an epic need within your family, community, nation, or world.

When all the laws of man declare that something God desires is impossible, the legendary woman reaches beyond the natural into the supernatural to believe the God of possibilities, because "with God all things are possible" (Matt. 19:26). God is freeing every woman from the prison of others' opinions, the fear of failure, and gender discrimination, especially within the body of Christ. It's time to embrace a new way of thinking. Jesus, the Lord of heaven, valued women when He walked the earth, and He values women now.

It's time to recognize the truth that the King of kings considers you His daughter, a precious jewel with value beyond measure. He has given you gifts and qualities specifically designed to help you fulfill your specific purpose. And even more importantly, He has given you the Holy Spirit to live inside you. It's time to embrace your kingdom assignment and rise up.

Your one simple yes to God can start you on the trajectory to creating a legendary legacy among women that lives on from generation to generation and forever changes the course of humankind.

THE LEGACY OF LEGENDS

God is activating in you and other women around the world the anointing of courage to carry the fullness of His promises. The world is in the midst of a global reset. God is aligning and reforming the earth. Wide-open doors of opportunity to preach the gospel and make the name of Jesus famous are presenting themselves. We can't back down; we must stand up. We can't step back; we must step up to the plate to establish and defend the standard of God-fearing, love-motivated leadership in the world. We are the very expression of God's rule and reign in feminine form.

Legendary women are legacy-minded women. They leave a legacy of bold, godly, loving leadership for their daughters. They leave a lasting imprint on the world through their faith, courage, compassion, wisdom, ingenuity, innovation, business acumen, and worship, and that imprint honors and magnifies the name of the Lord in every area of society.

The word *legend* traces back to the Latin word *legere*, meaning to gather, select, or read.[1] It was originally used in the Middle Ages to refer to stories about saints, which the faithful were duty bound to read. One author describes a legend as "whatever will come to be read by successive ages into an event or record of the past: the ever-new and ever-changing rereading of old sources by new generations."[2]

While legends are not limited to saints, the narratives, or legends, of people in the Bible were written for our admonishment and edification.

> For whatever was written in earlier times was written for our instruction, so that through endurance and the encouragement of the Scriptures we might have hope and overflow with confidence in His promises.
> —ROMANS 15:4, AMP

But the legends didn't stop with the saints named in the Bible. Throughout the ages men and women of God have continued to fulfill their callings, displaying great faith, great hope, and great love and inspiring others, whether on a grand scale or on a small one. And their legends are their legacies.

You may be thinking, "Michelle, I'm no saint." But that is not what the Word of God says.

> ...to those who are sanctified in Christ Jesus, called to be *saints*, with all who in every place call on the name of Jesus Christ our Lord.
> —1 CORINTHIANS 1:2, EMPHASIS ADDED

> Now, therefore, you are no longer strangers and foreigners, but fellow citizens with the *saints* and members of the household of God.
> —EPHESIANS 2:19, EMPHASIS ADDED

If you have called on the name of the Lord Jesus, if you are a citizen of the kingdom of God, if you are part of the body of Christ, you are a saint. That doesn't mean you have to fulfill the traditional, religious image of a saint, with a halo around your head. The Greek word translated "saints" simply means holy, or set apart.[3] When you determine to fulfill God's purpose for your life, it's like saying you agree to be a saint the way God defines it, meaning you are set apart for Him, exclusively His. Saints are just real-life, ordinary women (and men) who say yes to God.

And now is the time for a new generation of saints to answer the call, to be living legends through whom God is telling His story, using our stories of testing, trials, and triumph. The Bible tells us that our lives are legendary letters that should be read by the world.

> You yourselves are our letter of recommendation (our credentials), written in your hearts, to be known (perceived, recognized) and read by everybody. You show and make obvious that you are a letter from Christ delivered by us, not written with ink but with [the] Spirit of [the] living God, not on tablets of stone but on tablets of human hearts.
>
> —2 Corinthians 3:2–3, ampc

I want you to let this passage of Scripture marinate in your heart. God will use your life as a living letter to your generation. Your generosity, your obedience, your strength, and your love all attest to the goodness of God. Legendary women live their lives to bring glory to Jesus.

A legendary woman believes she can make a difference. A legendary woman doesn't pass the buck. Her strength and confidence come from finding her life and purpose in Jesus Christ. Empowered by her convictions, she is willing to lay down her selfish ambitions to champion the cause of Christ.

The legendary woman chooses purpose over popularity. She possesses both character and gifting, not one or the other like so many in the church today. She lives her life before an audience of One—the Lord God Almighty. She does not pledge her allegiance to any political system to advance her cause. She pledges her allegiance to her Lord and Savior, Jesus Christ, and the advancement of His kingdom.

There have been many bold and courageous women throughout history—in the Bible, in every age, in your own family, and all around you—who have believed God and obeyed Him, even when it cost them everything. You may already be numbered among those legendary women. But the truth is that we need legendary women now more than ever. We need women of fiery faith and obedience to believe God for the restoration of both male and female having dominion in the earth as one. Women will rule and reign in the earth alongside and in partnership with men, as God originally intended.

> Then God said, "Let Us make man in Our image, according to Our likeness; let *them* have dominion over the fish of the sea, over the birds of the air, and over the cattle, over all the earth and over every creeping thing that creeps on the earth." So God created man in His own image; in the image of God He created him; *male and female He created them.* Then God blessed *them,* and God said to *them,* "Be fruitful and multiply; fill the earth and subdue it; have dominion over the fish of the sea, over the birds of the air, and over every living thing that moves on the earth."
>
> —GENESIS 1:26–28, EMPHASIS ADDED

Legendary women will push forward with tenacious faith and the love of God so that the ancient war between men and women in the earth can finally end. Legendary women's displays of courage, character, and obedience will be passed on to their daughters and granddaughters, both natural and spiritual. So it is time to examine the legacy left to the legendary women of today by the legendary women of the past. Your spiritual inheritance includes so much more than you ever imagined.

CHARACTER TRAITS OF THE LEGENDARY WOMAN

> The word which came to Jeremiah from the LORD, saying: "Arise and go down to the potter's house, and there I will cause you to hear My words." Then I went down to the potter's house, and there he was, making something at the wheel. And the vessel that he made of clay was marred in the hand of the potter; so he made it again into another vessel, as it seemed good to the potter to make.
>
> Then the word of the LORD came to me, saying: "O house of Israel, can I not do with you as this potter?" says the LORD. "Look, as the clay is in the potter's hand, so are you in My hand, O house of Israel!"
>
> —JEREMIAH 18:1–6

I believe we are living in a critical time in human history. God is opening the hearts and minds of women to the possibility that they have the power to influence the world. God is shaping and developing the character of women to empower them to become living legends. He is taking the sensationalism out of what it means to be called by God. The call of God is a journey of encountering His presence; walking the path of righteousness; and discovering your inner strengths, your gifts, and the purpose for which you were created. The Lord as the master potter is revealing Himself to women. There is comfort in His hands-on approach in developing you. You are the clay in His loving hands.

Our wonderful Maker is carefully and purposefully positioning women in the center of His will for their lives. He is skillfully equipping us with the character traits needed to fulfill our callings. He is giving us a keen sense of discernment to recognize and capitalize on defining moments orchestrated by His providential hand. Woman of God, you and I must realize that we are fearfully and wonderfully made. We are the workmanship of the Lord, created for good works.

> I will praise You, for I am fearfully and wonderfully made; marvelous are Your works, and that my soul knows very well.
> —Psalm 139:14

> For we are His workmanship, created in Christ Jesus for good works, which God prepared beforehand that we should walk in them.
> —Ephesians 2:10

God is the potter, and we are the clay. His ways are so much higher than our ways (Isa. 55:9). His methods for molding and making us into vessels of honor are masterful. God uses both external and internal pressures in our lives to help shape us. Just as the potter chooses the type of clay for a unique vessel, God as the master designer has chosen you. He is truly working all things together for your good (Rom. 8:28). So don't curse your crisis. Don't belittle your experiences. Life can sometimes back you into a corner, but those defining moments reveal what you are truly made of. Your response to adversity reveals the true nature of who you are and what you are made of. And that is the very definition of *defining moment*: "the time that shows very clearly what something [or someone] is really about."[4]

The Lord has given mankind the beautiful gift of free will. He has granted you the dignity of choice. When making a decision, you must always begin with the heart and mind of God. You must seek His will and start with what is right according to the principles of the kingdom—not what is popular, comfortable, or socially acceptable. I admonish you to choose to stay under the mighty hand of God and let Him work in you "both to will and to do for His good pleasure" (Phil. 2:13).

Let the Lord develop in you the attributes needed to make your voice heard, to live a life of respect and honor that changes your world, to act according to His purpose for you, and to leave a legendary legacy of faith—with all of it being for the glory of God.

There are twelve character traits I have identified in legendary women. Some may possess only one or two, while others possess them all. The key is to use whatever traits you already have and allow God to develop the rest. Legendary women are marked by the following characteristics.

Filled with fiery faith

The legendary woman must develop a faith that is alive and tangible. When the deck is stacked against her and all natural possibilities are exhausted, the legendary woman will put her faith in the God who makes the impossible possible (Matt. 17:20; 19:26; Luke 1:37). As a legendary woman, you will find yourself in situations in which you must walk by faith and not sight (2 Cor. 5:7).

Courageous

A legendary woman trusts her gut and is courageous enough to take risks that advance the kingdom. At times this requires you to trust your relationship with the Lord and your ability to follow His leadership enough to challenge the status quo and push the envelope of earthly wisdom—even if it means putting your reputation or even your life on the line. Courage and bravery are like a two-edged sword that cuts off the head of every giant standing in the way of you and your destiny.

Fiercely loving and driven by compassion

Compassion is a driver that moves the legendary woman to take the risks necessary to secure lineages, legacies, whole cultures, and generations. Fierce love is the motivation behind the compassion. Love compels you to not merely ask, "If I don't save this one...clothe or feed this one...love this one, then who will?" but be the answer. The legendary woman understands that she is called to fiercely love beyond her comfort zone, so she will put herself on the line to serve and save others from harm and destruction.

Obedient

The legendary woman must develop a heart of obedience. Obedience is the lifeline of her existence. The Bible tells us that obedience is better than sacrifice (1 Sam. 15:22). More than any religious activity, the legendary woman must place a high value on doing what God tells her to do. If you're going to outsmart the devil and have unlimited access to the wisdom of God, obedience must be your highest goal. One act of obedience to God's command on the part of a legendary woman has the potential to save an entire family, community, or even nation from destruction.

Confrontational

The legendary woman will set a new precedent for what it means to pursue truth and justice, which means she will not hesitate to be confrontational when necessary. The legendary woman will not be afraid to confront issues that impede the cause of justice and righteousness. She will love truth, and she will have no qualms about asking for the truth. Her goal in this is not to be petty or arrogant but to face reality. She is willing to oppose an adversary, even if the enemy is within. The legendary woman will fearlessly be true to herself. She will also be willing to fight for truth and justice for others.

Skilled in the art of negotiation

A legendary woman never takes no for an answer when she is fulfilling her calling from God. Through her persistence the legendary woman will find a way over, around, or through any obstacle that may block the path forward. Through the power of the Holy Spirit she will discover how forcible the right words are. The legendary woman will speak up and challenge fears instead of letting fears challenge her. The beauty and brains of a legendary woman will bring some of the greatest solutions to some of the world's greatest challenges. The legendary woman will develop skills to play the win-win game of negotiation.

Discerning and wise

The legendary woman will cultivate a grace to understand the times and seasons of the Lord, seizing the opportunity for deliverance and protection for herself and her family. The legendary woman must tune in to her senses, especially the spiritual ones, and be aware of her surroundings and the changing times. By focusing on her divine assignment and purpose, the legendary woman will develop an ability to move with the Spirit of God and provide direction and quality leadership. She must know who she is and what she wants. She must be strategic, creative, and intentional in times of uncertainty. The legendary woman will arise with clarity and perceptiveness.

Extravagantly giving

God is giving the legendary woman power to get wealth to establish His covenant in the earth. There is a tremendous transference of wealth coming to the body of Christ through the business of the legendary woman. I believe the greatest inventions, cures, and financial savvy have been reserved for such a time as this. Philanthropy is a key trait for the legendary woman.

Poured out

The legendary woman has learned to be completely vulnerable to the Lord Jesus Christ. Through the grace of God she has determined to hold nothing back from service to her first love, Jesus. The sum total of her life is an act of worship to the Lord. Devotion is not expressed just in praise and worship songs but also in acts of kindness to others. The life of the legendary woman is broken open and poured on the feet of Jesus. Her time, talent, and resources belong completely to Him. Her quest is to have her life be a living sacrifice, and her passion for God is reflected in the words of the apostle Paul:

> But I will rejoice even if I lose my life, pouring it out like a liquid offering to God, just like your faithful service is an offering to God. And I want all of you to share that joy.
>
> —PHILIPPIANS 2:17, NLT

Stealthy in battle

The legendary woman knows she is in a battle, and she understands that actions speak louder than words. She knows that there is a time for words to stop and actions to begin. The legendary woman is strong when she is silent, and she is stealthy and accurate when it is time to act. This character trait allows the legendary woman to be a doer and not just a hearer of the Word (Jas. 1:22). There will be many assignments given to legendary women that are behind the scenes, but those assignments will lead to victory in battle for the Lord. Legendary women who are not looking for praise from others and who are willing to act silently and accurately are God's secret weapons.

Destiny driven

There is a purpose in the legendary woman's life that must be fulfilled. The legendary woman must realize that destiny is God's inner GPS, which leads, guides, pushes, and sometimes reroutes her toward His ordained purpose. The legendary woman understands that every aspect of her life matters to Jesus. She doesn't waste time and energy on frivolous things. Even when she has experienced some accomplishments or some misfortunes, there is an inner unction that keeps her moving toward God's eternal purposes for her life.

Victorious

The legendary woman is an overcomer. She holds on and keeps her hands to the plow until the job is done and the assignment is complete. The legendary woman will stop at nothing to accomplish the mission God has given her. She is not easily stopped by offense and won't hold grudges. She is a warrior, and because she has a discerning and wise heart, she understands her true enemy is the age-old one. He may bruise her, but through the power of the Holy Ghost she will crush him.

God has set the bar high for the legendary woman. He is redefining the meaning of greatness in our day. Greatness is not measured in dollars and cents. It is not measured by the applause of men. Jesus showed us that greatness is simply yet profoundly measured by our service to God and others.

One of my favorite scriptures is found in the Book of Acts. It states that David served his generation by the will of God (13:36). The greatest desire of a legendary woman is to serve her generation by the will of God. She is not trying to get accepted into good ole boys' clubs. She is creating and developing her own club. No longer is she looking for her greatness to come from the approval of those in authority.

The legendary woman's sole motivation is a desire to be legendary in the eyes of God. The legendary woman will not cower in fear of not being good enough. She is motivated by love for God and His creation. The driving force behind the legendary woman is bringing pleasure and glory to the Lord.

THE PROCESS

This book will walk you through what it means to possess each of these character traits, examining them through the narratives of both biblical legendary women and other legendary women of faith through the ages. They were women just like you and me, unassuming and living regular, everyday lives until they were faced with defining moments that changed everything—moments that made them legendary and examples to women today.

As you read, you will be empowered to give God your yes, and you will be equipped to faithfully fulfill the legendary role He has uniquely fashioned for you. You will be challenged and encouraged to consider your own defining moments and to dive deeper into who you really are in God. Prayers and declarations throughout will stir up the Spirit of God in you and compel you forward.

Woman of God, this is the hour when you must be led by the Spirit. This is the hour when you must be defined by what God says about you. This is the hour when you must be shrouded in a cloud of supernatural grace and power. God is strengthening you with power and might. You truly can do all things through Christ who strengthens and empowers you (Phil. 4:13).

PRAYER TO AWAKEN THE
LEGENDARY WOMAN IN YOU

God, I ask that You awaken the legendary woman inside of me. Let me see myself from Your perspective. You are the potter, and I am the clay. I yield to Your process of development. Remove everything that gets in the way of me believing You for the impossible. Break me free from the opinions of others. Break me free from the low opinion of myself. Lord, I ask that You release courage and bravery for me to live life according to Your calling for me. I accept the call to be awakened to a legendary destiny. Deliver me from every inner barrier. I repent of fear of people. I repent for not trusting You and instead trusting the arm of flesh. Father, I embrace Your will for my life. I place my hand in Your loving hand and trust Your plan for me. Lord, I ask You for a plan of action. Teach me how to embrace my call. Help me recognize every defining moment. Destroy every belief system that has crippled me in my calling. I desire to be a woman of conviction, influence, and power. I desire to be legendary for Your glory.

DECLARATIONS TO AFFIRM THE LEGENDARY WOMAN IN YOU

I am a living legend.

I inspire.

I live my life before an audience of one.

The Lord is my portion.

God's will for my life is my one desire.

I live to please God and God alone.

I will leave a legacy for the next generation.

My life is important.

I am a world-changing woman.

I will live a world-changing life.

I will change the world one soul at a time.

I will leave a legacy of obedience to the will of God.

I am not divided in my desire.

I will serve my generation by the will of God.

I loose myself from the opinions of others.

I will not be defined by my success or failure.

I am defined by what the Lord says about me.

The Lord says I am loved.

I will walk in courage.

I will be bold in my speech.

I am a fierce lover of Jesus.

I am a woman of compassion.

I have fiery faith.

I will be obedient and die to myself.

I will take up my cross daily.

I will pursue truth.

I will confront injustice.

I am a master negotiator.

I am discerning and wise.

I am an extravagant giver.

I will be obedient to the call and purpose of God.

I am a legendary woman.

PART I

Becoming a Living Legend

Chapter 1

BELIEVING GOD FOR THE IMPOSSIBLE

Legendary Women Are Filled With Fiery Faith

Faith sees the invisible, believes the unbelievable,
and receives the impossible.
—CORRIE TEN BOOM

L EGENDARY WOMEN POSSESS fiery faith in God. Fiery
faith is a faith that's alive. Fiery faith in God consumes
doubt and unbelief. The fiery faith of a legendary woman
ignites and empowers everyone around her. Her fierce faith in
the impossible, the unfounded, and the unbelievable is the stuff
of legends. She knows there isn't anything that is too hard for
the Lord (Gen. 18:14) and that "with God all things are possible" (Matt. 19:26). She has a hunger for the Word because
she knows that "faith comes by hearing, and hearing by the
word of God" (Rom. 10:17). She knows that her devotional
life—reading, studying, and meditating on the Word of God
for herself with the help of the Holy Spirit, not just listening
to sermons or reading Christian books—is critical to her faith.

But what is faith? The Word of God tells us faith "is the
substance of things hoped for, the evidence of things not seen"
(Heb. 11:1). The Greek word is *pistis*, which means persuasion,
moral conviction, assurance, and belief. It means the "conviction of the truth...respecting man's relationship to God."[1]
Faith means you are convinced and assured that God is exactly
who He says He is and that His promises are true. I love the
way the Passion Translation puts it: "Faith brings our hopes

into reality and becomes the foundation needed to acquire the things we long for. It is all the evidence required to prove what is still unseen. This testimony of faith is what previous generations were commended for. Faith empowers us to see that the universe was created and beautifully coordinated by the power of God's words! He spoke and the invisible realm gave birth to all that is seen" (Heb. 11:1–3).

Those are the verses that open the passage of Scripture known as the Hall of Faith, the testimonies of faith passed down as a legacy to us. It speaks of Abel, whose faith moved him to choose a more acceptable sacrifice and be declared righteous (v. 4); the faith of Enoch, who never experienced death "because God promoted him" in response to the pleasure He found in him (v. 5, TPT); Noah, whose heart was opened by faith to receive divine warning and revelation of "even things that had never been seen" and to receive "God's gift of righteousness that comes by believing" (v. 6–7, TPT); and the faith that caused Abraham to obey God and leave "with only a promise" on a journey to discover his inheritance (v. 8, TPT). It speaks of faith that inspired, operated powerfully, opened eyes, enabled people to choose God's will, stirred people up, opened the way, pulled down walls, conquered kingdoms, established justice, shut the mouths of lions, put out raging fires, and sparked courage (vv. 17–34).

And this is the faith of the legendary woman. Her faith pleases the Lord. It enables her to receive revelation. It allows her to operate powerfully in the gifts God has given her. It inspires her, opens her eyes, stirs her up, and sparks courage. The faith of the legendary woman tears down walls, whether physical, mental, or spiritual. The faith of the legendary woman puts out fires and conquers kingdoms. This is your faith, woman of God. It is the faith that grabs on to God's promises and pulls them into reality (Heb. 11:33, TPT).

And just as Enoch's faith pleased God, your faith pleases

God. In fact you can't please God without it (Heb. 11:6). Faith is also a fruit of the Spirit (Gal. 5:22). Notice that Galatians says, "The fruit of the Spirit is...," not "The fruits of the Spirit are..." That means the fruit of the Spirit is all or nothing. If you have the Holy Spirit, you have faith along with all the other qualities that are part of the fruit of the Spirit.

Faith is also a gift (1 Cor. 12:4–10; Eph. 2:8). It is a free gift, given to you by God out of His grace. And this gift is activated by believing in your heart and confessing with your mouth (Rom. 10:9–10).

Faith is also what gives you access to God:

> Therefore, having been justified by faith, we have peace with God through our Lord Jesus Christ, through whom also we have access by faith into this grace in which we stand, and rejoice in hope of the glory of God.
>
> —ROMANS 5:1–2

The word translated "access" means the act of bringing to, access, approach, or admission.[2] That means faith is heaven's currency. It gives you free admission to approach the throne of God. It gives you unlimited access to the Lord Most High so that you can go "boldly to the throne of grace, that [you] may obtain mercy and find grace to help in time of need" (Heb. 4:16). And knowing that you have that access and knowing the power behind the gift of faith God has given you will help you overcome the biggest hindrance to faith: fear.

Matthew 8 tells of a time when Jesus and the disciples were crossing the sea and a big storm came up. When the disciples reacted in fear, Jesus asked them, "Why are you fearful, O you of little faith?" (v. 26). Fear decreases your faith. It makes it little. But when you recognize, as the disciples did just a moment after Jesus asked them that question, that God is in control, no matter the size or strength of the storm, your faith will rise up and your fear will not stand a chance. Don't let fear hinder your faith. Your faith may be under development at this juncture in your life, but remember, you are the rich inheritance of generations of men and women whose lives provide road maps to you embracing and growing in your faith. Your faith gives you free admission to the throne of grace, and even the wind and waves obey the One who sits on that throne.

A FOUNDATION OF FAITH

Just as Hebrews says faith is "the foundation needed to acquire the things we long for" (11:1, TPT), it is also the foundation of all the character traits of the legendary woman. They all start with faith. So faith is where the legendary woman starts. Faith in God is what causes a legendary woman to stand. The legendary woman understands that it is in Him that she lives and moves and has her being. She lives her life with a sense of urgency to fulfill her mandate to make the name of Jesus famous.

The legendary woman knows what she is made of. She knows that it is easy to stand in faith when things are going well, but she also knows that she will stand in faith when things get hard. In the face of the crisis she will raise up her shield of faith to vanquish the fiery darts of the enemy (Eph. 6:16). And just as Roman soldiers could link their shields to create an impenetrable wall, she knows there are times when she will be called upon to link her shield of faith with the shields of other legendary women in the midst of fierce battle, and she will do so boldly and courageously, knowing that God is for her (Rom. 8:31). She knows that "all the promises of God in Him are Yes, and in Him Amen, to the glory of God" (2 Cor. 1:20).

The legendary woman's faith undergirds her ability to "watch, stand fast in the faith, be brave, be strong" (1 Cor. 16:13). Her faith brings stability to her mind and spirit since it brings the peace that passes all understanding and guards her heart and mind through Jesus (Phil. 4:7). Fear will not have dominion over the legendary woman because her faith is unshakable—it kicks fear to the curb.

The legendary woman's faith also keeps her moving. It propels her forward. She knows there is a calling on her life, and she has the faith to fulfill it. She steps out in faith, going where God commands and wholeheartedly pursuing His purposes for her life. She is willing, like Abraham, to obey and move toward the new territory God has for her "with only a promise" (Heb. 11:8, TPT), because she knows the One she has faith in, and she is convinced that He is willing and able to keep His word (2 Tim. 1:12).

The legendary woman acts on her faith because she knows faith without works is dead (Jas. 2:17). Her faith will not allow fear to make her hesitate, stall, delay, or stop in the fulfillment of her heavenly calling. Because of the access to the throne room of heaven that faith has given her, she petitions God in faith, moves with God in faith, and receives His favor. And because her faith is so fiery, it ignites faith in others, creating a blaze of light that is a city on a hill that cannot be hidden (Matt. 5:14). And that faith is part of her legacy, which is passed down to her natural and spiritual children and grandchildren, from generation to generation.

THE FAITH OF SARAH

The legendary woman's legacy of faith can be traced back to legends of the Bible. I always say if God did anything through anyone at any time in history, He could do it through me! Let's take a look at the legendary women included in the Hall of Faith. The women named in that chapter left us a profound legacy of fierce, fiery faith. The first woman mentioned in Hebrews 11 is Sarah.

> Sarah's faith embraced God's miracle power to conceive even though she was barren and was past the age of childbearing, for the authority of her faith rested in the One who made the promise, and she tapped into his faithfulness. In fact, so many children were subsequently fathered by this aged man of faith—one who was as good as dead, that he now has offspring as innumerable as the sand on the seashore and as the stars in the sky!
> —HEBREWS 11:11–12, TPT

When God promised she would have a son, Sarah was ninety years old, decades past normal child-bearing years, and Abraham was no spring chicken. Because of her age and how long she had been barren, I can understand why Sarah's first reaction when she overheard the Lord saying she would have a son was to laugh to herself, saying, "After I have grown old, shall I have pleasure, my lord being old also?" (Gen. 18:12). But then came what I think was Sarah's defining moment of faith, when the Lord asked, "Is anything too hard for the LORD?" (v. 14). It was the moment that her faith rose up to believe that the One who promised them a son is faithful. She "embraced God's miracle power" and "tapped into his faithfulness" (Heb. 11:11, TPT). The truth that nothing is impossible for God resonated deep within her and stirred up the faith that would allow her to conceive a son. Only the Lord can ask you a question that shifts your focus from natural, carnal reasoning. When you are faced with the seemingly impossible, God is releasing in you the ability to rise up and tap into the faithfulness of God, just as Sarah did, and embrace the supernatural moving of the hand of God in your life. Don't let fear keep you barren. Stir up your faith to conceive the fulfillment of the promises of God in your life.

The Lord keeps His promises. He kept His promise to Sarah and Abraham, and He will keep His promises to you. The Lord returned to Sarah at the appointed time, and she had a baby. The result of her faith was life, and not only for Isaac but also for all his descendants, who number more than the stars in the sky. And when "the authority of [your] faith [rests] in the One who made the promise" (Heb. 11:11, TPT), the Lord will also return to you at the appointed time, allowing you to birth the fulfillment of His promises to you.

THE FAITH OF RAHAB

The other woman mentioned by name in the Hall of Faith is Rahab:

> By faith the harlot Rahab did not perish with those who did not believe, when she had received the spies with peace.
>
> —HEBREWS 11:31

Just as with Sarah, the result of Rahab's faith was life. Rahab ran a brothel in Jericho. The two spies Joshua sent to check out the city stayed at her house. The king of Jericho found out about them and asked Rahab to give them up. But then came her defining moment of faith. Instead of turning the spies over to the king, she hid them on the roof, telling the king that the spies had already left. She explained her reasoning to the spies:

> I know that the LORD has given you the land, that the terror of you has fallen on us, and that all the inhabitants of the land are fainthearted because of you. For we have heard how the LORD dried up the water of the Red Sea for you when you came out of Egypt, and what you did to the two kings of the Amorites who were on the other side of the Jordan, Sihon and Og, whom you utterly destroyed. And as soon as we heard these things, our hearts melted; neither did there remain any more

> courage in anyone because of you, for the LORD your
> God, He is God in heaven above and on earth beneath.
> —JOSHUA 2:9–11

Rahab knew that the Lord was God because of the stories she had heard. She knew that the One who could do all those things had to be the real deal, the one true God of heaven and earth. And Rahab's story demonstrates how powerful your story, your testimony, is. Stories of the goodness and faithfulness of God stir up faith in others, even unbelievers. Rahab's faith was stirred because of what she heard, and because of her faith not only did the two spies live, but Rahab and all her relatives were spared when the Israelites conquered Jericho. From then on, Rahab lived in Israel, even marrying a man from the tribe of Judah. Put another way, "Faith provided a way of escape for Rahab the prostitute" (Heb. 11:31, TPT).

Rahab was facing a changing world. She could have allowed her social status as a prostitute to keep her silent in shame, but she used her intuition to see the open door of opportunity for a new life. She could have chosen to act in fear, but instead she chose to act in faith. And her faith provided a way to escape. It provided a way through, a way out, a new way. Just like Rahab, the legendary women of today are facing a changing world. We live in a world of chaos and COVID, racism and riots, and countless other things that can stir up fear.

But, legendary woman, it's time for you to stir up your faith, not your fear. Your faith will provide a way. Jesus said, "I am the way" (John 14:6). And He is the way. He will provide a way to escape, a way through, a way out, a new way for you. He will "instruct you and teach you in the way you should go" (Ps. 32:8). Because of your faith, "your ears shall hear a word behind you, saying, 'This is the way, walk in it,' whenever you turn to the right hand or whenever you turn to the left" (Isa. 30:21). And the Lord's way is "the way which leads to life" (Matt. 7:14).

Faith leads to life. Your faith results in life—and not just any kind of life, but abundant life. Both Sarah's and Rahab's faith resulted in life. But it goes even deeper than just the immediate results of the rescue of Rahab and her family or Isaac's birth or even the innumerable descendants of Isaac. Both Sarah and Rahab were direct ancestors of Jesus. Rahab is actually one of the few women named in Jesus' genealogy in the Gospel of Matthew (1:5). Jesus came that we might have life and have it more abundantly (John 10:10). He came that we might have eternal life (John 3:15; 17:3). By stepping up with fiery faith to fulfill the calling of God for their lives, Sarah and Rahab played a part in making that life possible.

RESURRECTING FAITH

While Sarah and Rahab are the only women mentioned by name in the Hall of Faith, other women are included:

> Women received their dead raised to life again.
> —HEBREWS 11:35

This verse intrigues me. Women received their dead raised to life. Their actions spoke louder than words. Their acts of faith made them legendary—not their names or pedigrees, not their degrees or talents, not their social class or their wealth, but their simple, childlike faith. Once again, the result of fiery faith is life. The verse is likely referring to women such as the widow of Zarephath, whose son was raised from the dead by Elijah (1 Kings 17:17–22), and the Shunnamite woman, whose son was raised from the dead by Elisha (2 Kings 4:17–37). Both women exhibited great faith, with the Shunnamite woman even declaring, "It is well," several times after the death of her son. For both women, their defining moments came when they chose to believe that even though death had occurred, resurrection to life was possible.

Legendary women of fiery faith are women who believe that "with God all things are possible" (Matt. 19:26), even physically raising someone from the dead. I am reminded of a movie called *Breakthrough*, highlighting Joyce Smith's defining moment of faith, which came while she was in a hospital room with her fourteen-year-old son. He had fallen through an icy lake in Missouri and had been underwater for fifteen minutes and without a pulse for more than forty minutes after being pulled from the frigid water. The ER doctor wrote, "I had exhausted all interventions in my scientific armamentarium without even a hint of success. All the resources of this world were being thrust upon this young man with no indication except the cold reality of a young life snuffed out before our very eyes."[3] But Joyce wasn't putting her faith in modern medicine to save her son.

With her hands on her son's ice-cold feet, she stirred up her fiery faith and declared in a voice loud enough to be heard all across the ER, "I believe in a God who can do miracles! Holy Spirit, I need You right now to come and breathe life back into my son!"[4] And that is exactly what happened. Her son's heart started to beat again. He was raised to life after being dead for almost an hour. The ER doctor acknowledged, "The Holy Spirit came in that room and started that boy's heart once again."[5]

But I think Hebrews 11:35, "Women received their dead raised to life again," can speak to more than just physical resurrection. I believe it speaks to the kind of faith legendary women have to bring those who are spiritually dead to life. I believe spiritual resurrection is just as powerful as physical resurrection because people who die in their sins are lost forever, for all eternity.

> But God, who is rich in mercy, because of His great love with which He loved us, even when we were dead in trespasses, made us alive together with Christ (by grace you have been saved), and raised us up together, and made us

sit together in the heavenly places in Christ Jesus, that
in the ages to come He might show the exceeding riches
of His grace in His kindness toward us in Christ Jesus.

—EPHESIANS 2:4–7

The legendary woman has fiery faith to believe that her
dead—the unsaved among her family and friends—will be
made alive with Christ. She believes they will become new cre-
ations, with the old passing away and all things becoming new
(2 Cor. 5:17). She won't stop believing and praying and asking
and knocking and seeking until her prodigals come home. She
knows what it is like to have abundant life here on earth, and
she wants others to experience it too. But above all she wants
the assurance of eternal life for those she loves. So she will
raise her shield of faith. She will go boldly before the throne
of grace to find help in times of need. She will remind God of
His promises, and she will stand on the knowledge that God is
faithful and keeps His promises. Fear won't stop her. Despair
won't stop her. She will watch. She will stand fast. She will be
brave. She will be strong. She will overcome. And she will see
her dead raised to life again.

YOUR DEFINING MOMENT

Woman of God, you possess a precious legacy of fiery faith
that has been passed down from legendary woman to legendary
woman, from generation to generation. It is time to take up
that mantle and begin to exercise legendary faith! God's Word
says that faith without works is dead (Jas. 2:20)! What dream
has God given you? As with what happened to Rahab, the
world we were born into has changed, and now we need the
faith to pivot in a new direction.

Through the eyes of faith, Rahab engineered a deal that
saved her family. I want you to note that Rahab was not sanc-
tified, had not read a lot of Bible verses, and had not attended

29

any church services; she had only heard about the awesomeness of God and believed. Faith provided her a way to escape and avoid destruction. God is awakening faith in your heart—faith to receive revelation and warning that will preserve your legacy.

If you are going to complete your calling, you must take a new look at Jesus.

> Looking unto Jesus, the author and finisher of our faith.
> —HEBREWS 12:2

Jesus is the perfect example of legendary faith. You must focus your gaze on Him. You must give Him your undivided attention. God is raising up women whose legendary faith will grab hold of the promises of God and pull them into reality.

The ultimate goal of faith is abundant life here on earth and eternal life in heaven with Jesus. And you will leave behind a legacy of faith as well. What will that legacy look like? What will be your defining moment?

Defining moments of faith are never easy. They come when life is difficult. They come when things seem to not make sense. Elisabeth Elliot, a legendary woman of fiery faith, wrote, "Faith's most severe tests come not when we see nothing, but when we see a stunning array of evidence that seems to prove our faith vain."[6] Jesus also warned us that "difficult is the way which leads to life" (Matt. 7:14). No one wants to face testing and trials, but the truth is that they develop and strengthen your faith. So take James' advice and "count it all joy," keeping your eye on the prize: "that you may be perfect and complete, lacking nothing" (Jas. 1:2–4).

Think of trials as exercise for your faith. Your faith is like a muscle. If you don't use it and stretch it, it weakens. The legendary woman knows she must exercise her faith. The Bible encourages:

> But you, beloved, building yourselves up on your most holy faith, praying in the Holy Spirit, keep yourselves in

the love of God, looking for the mercy of our Lord Jesus
Christ unto eternal life.

—JUDE 20–21

Build yourself in faith! Pray in the Holy Spirit. Give your
faith a workout! Use it every day. Practice raising that shield
of faith so when your defining moment comes, you can raise it
high without effort. Read the Word. Dig into it. Meditate on
it. Write it on the tablet of your heart. Remember that faith
comes by hearing the Word of God. The Word is vital to the
fiery faith of a legendary woman.

Your faith is a gift from God, and it is a powerful gift. It
moves mountains. It breaks through barriers. It pulls down walls.
It shuts the mouths of lions. It gives courage. It conquers kingdoms. It parts seas. It imparts power and makes you strong. And
you need to keep hold of it until your race is finished. God has
called you for a purpose, and He has given you the faith needed
to fulfill that purpose. So don't keep your shield of faith hanging
there at your side like a useless weight. Raise it up!

And when your defining moment comes, you will be ready.
It may be a moment like that of the widow of Zarephath or
Joyce Smith, when you are contending for the physical life of
someone you love. It may be a moment when your prodigal is
so far away and so far gone that everything seems hopeless, but
you raise your mighty shield of faith, contending for spiritual
resurrection. It may be a moment when the world expects your
circumstances to leave you dismal and despairing. But remem-
bering that the joy of the Lord is your strength, you will rise up
in faith, declaring for all to hear that the promises of God are
yes and amen, to the glory of God! Your faith will arise, backed
by the power of the Lord God Almighty. You will speak words
of life and see the Lord bring them to pass. You will be a legendary woman of fiery faith, and your story of the triumph of
faith in the midst of trials will be your legacy.

Prayer for Breakthrough Faith

Father, 2 Corinthians 5:7 says, "For we walk by faith, not by sight." I choose to live by faith, not by what I can or cannot see with the natural eye. I will view my life from Your perspective. Let the eyes of faith impart prophetic vision for the future. Open the eyes of my spirit to see You. Open the eyes of my heart to know and live by Your promises. I want to see and know You more. By faith let me experience You working in me and around me. Lord, I want to fulfill my assignment in the earth. I choose to trust and believe in Your unseen presence more than the natural temporal realm.

Father, I believe that You are God! I come diligently seeking You for a greater measure of faith. I ask that You increase my faith. There is nothing too hard for You. I know without faith it is impossible to please You. I believe and judge You faithful! You are a rewarder of those who diligently seek You. I will hold on to every promise You've spoken over my life. Lord, I ask that You increase my faith for my assignment. Let my faith come alive. I desire to have fiery faith in the impossible, the unfounded, and what mankind calls unbelievable. You have given every man a measure of faith. I ask that You will cause my measure to grow daily.

"And my speech and my preaching were not with persuasive words of human wisdom, but in demonstration of the Spirit and of power, that your faith should not be in the wisdom of men but in the power of God" (1 Cor. 2:4–5).

DECLARATIONS TO BUILD FIERY FAITH

I will leave a legacy of fiery faith.

I look to Jesus, the author and finisher of my faith.

Jesus, You are the perfect example of faith.

My testimony will be that I pleased God.

I will not be a man pleaser but a God pleaser.

I will live from the realm of faith.

I will not allow doubt and unbelief to confine me to this temporal, passing-away realm. Just like the legendary women of Hebrews 11 who lived their lives on earth as those who belonged to another realm, so will I.

My faith will activate angelic assistance.

My faith will conquer and will establish justice.

My faith will not only look at the immediate but see the ultimate reward of life.

My faith will believe God to cross Red Seas of my life.

I decree my faith will move mountains.

I decree my faith in God will embrace the miracle power to conceive and birth the purposes of God, regardless of my age.

I decree that I have authority because I believe God to be faithful.

In my weakness, faith imparts power to make me strong.

I decree breakthrough faith!

Chapter 2

BRAVE HEARTS

Legendary Women Are Courageous

Being courageous isn't about pretending that bad
things don't happen or that real risks are all in our head.
Being courageous is being honest with what we are
facing and feeling then pushing on.

—BETHANY HAMILTON

I CALL THE LEGENDARY woman Braveheart. She has the
mental and moral strength to show courage in any situation. Her heart knows that the opposite of fear is love
and that "perfect love drives out fear" (1 John 4:18, NASB). Her
encounters with God free her from fear, even the fear of death.
She is fueled by conviction activated in the presence of God.
The visitation of the Lord awakens zeal in her soul, creating a
holy dissatisfaction with complacency. She possesses a divine
urgency to will and to do of the pleasure of the Lord, and that
urgency gives her the courage to speak the truth of the Word
boldly, to love fiercely, to give extravagantly, to act accurately,
to be poured out fully, and to overcome victoriously.

The legendary woman lives by a code of conviction that places
the will of God and His written Word as the final authority
in her life. Her tenacious faith in the Lord of her assignment
is the birthplace of her courage. The legendary woman has a
strength of mind and spirit that enables her to face difficulty.
Her heart compels her to stand for justice and truth, even in
the face of unpopular opinion. She will go against the grain to
save the innocent. The legendary woman will never conform to

the status quo out of fear, rejection, or the need for approval because she has encountered the King of glory.

DEFINING COURAGE

Merriam-Webster defines *courage* as "mental or moral strength to venture, persevere, and withstand danger, fear, or difficulty."[1] Courage encompasses strength of mind, strength of heart, and strength of spirit. It gives the legendary woman the ability to persevere in the face of any difficulties and dangers that would keep her from pursuing her God-given purpose. And keep in mind that the legendary woman's strength of heart is not the same as hardness of heart. Hardness of heart—which can be caused by things such as bitterness, anger, habitual sin, rebellion, and pride—is a hindrance to having a brave heart. The legendary woman's strength comes from the Lord, and it makes her heart anything but hard. The legendary woman's continual prayer is "God, give me Your heart for my assignment!"

The Hebrew word translated "courage" in well-known passages, such as Deuteronomy 31 and Joshua 1, that encourage us to be strong and of good courage is *'amats*, meaning strong, alert, established, steadfastly minded, brave, courageous, and bold.[2] The legendary woman knows her strength comes from the Lord, and that enables her to be steadfastly minded, knowing that the Lord will establish her steps and give her the bravery and boldness needed to see her assignments through until the end.

Jehosheba was a legendary woman who personified this trait. This brave-hearted woman was directed by righteous indignation and a passion for justice. Shaking with both righteous anger and fleshly fear, she leaped forward with courage and bravery to rescue her nephew from the murderous plot of his grandmother Athaliah to execute him. Many times, fulfilling the call of God starts right in your own family. Women are faced with defining moments within their families all the time, from struggling to keep a marriage together to trying not to go crazy raising young children to having to raise grandchildren because their parents made bad choices.

Jehosheba was a heroic aunt who rescued her nephew and gave up years of her life to provide for and shelter him. These acts of kindness remind me of my story. My mom died when I was four years old, and I never knew my father. I was raised by my grandmother. She never plotted to kill me, although my stubbornness and my fight for independence in my teenage years may have tempted her a few times. Yet our personalities clashed so much that I eventually ran away. My aunt Nomia stepped in and made room for me in her family to live with her from my teenage years to adulthood. The street life in Chicago could have swallowed me whole. If it wasn't for her legendary act of courage, I might not even be alive and writing this book right now. She sheltered and provided for me, just as Jehosheba did for her nephew Joash.

UNSEEN BY THE WORLD BUT SEEN BY GOD

The story of Jehosheba (also called Jehoshabeath) can be found in 2 Kings 11 and 2 Chronicles 22. She was a legendary woman whose heroic acts are often unsung in biblical teachings. I must admit, I really hadn't known of her story until I started doing research for this book. Thanks be unto God that He knows and rewards every unseen action of our lives. Jehosheba is a perfect example of a sacrifice made in secret that God sees and rewards openly (Matt. 6:4). Because of her heroic act, the Messianic bloodline can be traced through Solomon.[3] History credits her with saving the royal seed of David from extinction. She is a perfect example of a godly woman who, in the midst of murder, idolatry, and nail-biting fear, rose above her sense of self-preservation to do what was right. That is what legendary women do. They rise above the fear to do what is right, to fulfill the calling of God in their lives.

Jehosheba's act of courage was orchestrated by the providence of God and fulfilled His promise to David that his seed would forever sit on the throne (2 Sam. 7:16; Ps. 89:35–37). Here's her story:

> When Athaliah the mother of Ahaziah saw that her son was dead, she arose and destroyed all the royal heirs. But Jehosheba, the daughter of King Joram, sister of Ahaziah, took Joash the son of Ahaziah, and stole him away from among the king's sons who were being murdered; and they hid him and his nurse in the bedroom, from Athaliah, so that he was not killed. So he was hidden with her in the house of the LORD for six years, while Athaliah reigned over the land. In the seventh year Jehoiada sent and brought the captains of hundreds—of the bodyguards and the escorts—and brought them into the house of the LORD to him. And he made a covenant with them and took an oath from them in the house of the LORD, and showed them the king's son.
>
> —2 KINGS 11:1–4

Jehosheba was the daughter of Joram, also known as Jehoram, who was king of Judah. She was the sister of Ahaziah, the king of Judah whose death was referred to in the first verse of 2 Kings 11. But Jehosheba was certainly not a product of her environment. Her father, Joram, did evil in the sight of the Lord. Joram was a wicked king who was influenced by his wicked wife, Athaliah, who was the daughter of Jezebel, one of the most notoriously wicked women of all time (2 Kings 8:16–18). Athaliah, taking a cue from her mother's example, was the epitome of greed and lust for power. The legacy Athaliah inherited was one of wickedness and idolatry.

But Jehosheba had a righteous heart for the Lord. She chose not to accept the legacy of wickedness being passed down through her bloodline. She was what I call a bloodline curse breaker. Jehosheba rebelled against her lineage of evil and iniquity to serve the true and living God. Even in a kingdom that was full of idolatry, she kept her focus on the Lord. This is the heart of the legendary woman. We must not allow our family environments to influence our life decisions! It doesn't matter what side of the tracks you come from. Don't be afraid to do something different. Don't be afraid to take a risk. Legendary women are risk takers and history makers. Jehosheba's one act of bravery started a reformation in her family bloodline. Great reforms often begin with one person!

Jehosheba was married to the high priest, Jehoiada, who had a reputation for being godly and steadfast in his service to the Lord. It could be that Jehosheba's marriage helped develop her heart to serve the Lord. Jehosheba's husband was a man of authority who worked to restore worship of the Lord rather than Baal in Israel (2 Kings 11:17–18). Together Jehosheba and Jehoiada hid Joash from Athaliah for six years. They truly were a power couple who demonstrated that two are better than one (Eccles. 4:9).

The meaning of Jehoiada's name, "Jehovah knows," has a clear connection to the man and his character.[4] And Jehosheba's name also speaks a profound truth about her character. It means "Jehovah has sworn" or "whose oath is Jehovah," the implication of the latter being the Lord Most High was the One she was swearing by and was therefore the One she chose to worship.[5] The legendary woman must partner with God to fulfill her call. He knows you and is always with you.

Jehosheba's choice to worship God was likely not an easy one. Can you imagine living in a time of extreme immorality and ritualistic worship? Can you imagine what it would be like if most of your family members, including your parents and siblings, were caught up in idolatry and all the sin that comes with it? Jehosheba didn't have a Bible to read or a pastor to teach and disciple her. She was living in a time when much compromise and perversion prevailed, yet she still managed to do the right thing. We are also living in a time of compromise and perversion, yet as legendary women we need to rise up and do the right thing. We need to have the courage to go against the flow toward wickedness and take a stand for righteousness in this generation.

Now imagine that your brother, who has been king since your father died, passes away. And his mother, who is either your mother or your stepmother, decides she wants to be the next monarch of the kingdom. In order to achieve that, all the potential royal heirs must die, and so a massacre begins at the palace. All your nephews, regardless of their age, are being murdered because of one woman's lust for power. Can you imagine what it would be like to hear screams and cries for help ringing through the royal palace?

Now I want you to fast-forward to the year 2020 and beyond. Can you hear the cries of creation groaning for you to fulfill your assignment? Just as the royal palace halls were filled with cries for help, our society is crying out for help. One of the major spirits that attacks the brave heart is hardness of heart. The aftermath of coronavirus, racial riots, and police brutality has left the souls of our nation overcome by pain and fear. Are you willing to keep a soft heart? Are you willing to pray and ask the Lord to take out your heart of stone and give you a new heart of flesh and a new spirit (Ezek. 36:26)? Are you willing to step forward with courage and bravery to fulfill your assignment to bring peace, healing, and restoration? Jehosheba stepped in to save the next generation. Is that the dream God has put in your heart? Perhaps God has given you a vision to create a school for young and gifted legendary women. Is this your moment to act in faith and be a legendary woman who answers the cries for help?

I imagine that as the massacre began, Jehosheba's heart was both pounding because of fear and breaking because of grief.

The adrenaline and shock must have made her want to look away, to run away, to hide herself from the horror of what was happening. But then Jehosheba had her defining moment.

Instead of continuing to watch the massacre or hiding her face in fear, Jehosheba decided to act. Legendary woman, it's not until you make the decision to act that the grace of God will be released. Perhaps Joash was the last on the list to be killed since he was just a baby and couldn't run away or hide on his own. Perhaps he was the only one small enough for Jehosheba to get out of harm's way. Whatever the circumstances, Jehosheba risked her own life to save the life of her nephew, who had just become the rightful king of Judah because of the death of all the other heirs. Jehosheba truly had a brave heart. The presence of mind it took to rescue her nephew and hide him demonstrates what real women, what legendary women, are made of. This legendary woman was bold and courageous.

TAKE COURAGE!

In Matthew 14:27 Jesus admonished us, "Take courage!...Don't be afraid" (NIV). *Take courage* is an action phrase. You need to *take* it and choose not to be afraid! There are times in life when your faith has to jump over your fear. Courage has to be taken! It's a proactive step. It requires your permission. It requires your choice.

Jehosheba chose to be courageous despite social disapproval and despite the potential danger to herself. Courage does not deny the existence of danger; it denies the power of danger over your life. Courage denies the power of fear to keep you from fulfilling your calling. Remember, "God has not given us a spirit of fear, but of power and of love and of a sound mind" (2 Tim. 1:7).

I believe Jehosheba's courage was developed over time as she chose to live virtuously in her day-to-day life, even when surrounded by people who seemed to be getting ahead despite their wickedness. This is one of the challenges we face today as legendary women. Our society is flooded with people who seem to be getting ahead even though they curse God and rob the innocent, but the legendary woman still chooses righteousness. She still chooses to do what is right in the eyes of the Lord instead of what is popular or easy or seemingly more advantageous. And the legendary woman must not be afraid to be a rebel against unfair systems that devour the next generation.

Most assignments from God are not over in a matter of moments, so it is important to develop courage that endures. I am convinced that God has placed in each person a seed of righteousness, and He allows each of us to choose how we will live. It is those everyday choices that will develop your character, for better or for worse. Choosing righteousness every day and making right decisions create momentum that moves you closer to impacting the world and bringing glory to God. And the truth is that God's grace—if you take the time to notice it—is gently wooing you to make righteous life choices. It's the kindness of God that leads you to repentance (Rom. 2:4). And making godly choices on a day-to-day basis keeps your heart from being hardened by sin, the dangers of which are clearly seen in Jehosheba's story.

Jehosheba and Athaliah are a perfect contrast between selflessness and selfishness. Their lives were polar opposites. Jehosheba was a godly woman who preserved a generation. Athaliah was a wicked, unsanctified woman who attacked and destroyed almost an entire generation of a family by murdering the royal heirs. Athaliah's heart was so hard that she murdered her own grandchildren for her own selfish gain. Jehosheba's heart was so soft yet strong that she selflessly risked her life for her nephew out of love.

Prophetically I want you to see that we can have a little of both women's character in our makeup. We must allow the Holy Spirit to reveal and remove anything in our DNA that will give way to selfishness. Legendary women must take up the cross daily. We must die to ourselves, as John 12:24 admonishes. Death to self produces much fruit. Selfishness—living only for yourself—can detour your life's purpose. Death to self starts with a decision. You must decide to give up your right to be right. You must make a decision to be righteous.

Jehosheba's heart needed to be strong because she didn't need courage just in the moment; she needed courage that endured. Joash was hidden in the house of the Lord for six years, and it wasn't until the seventh year that he was brought out and crowned king. Her assignment wasn't completed until the seventh year, and she had to maintain her courage the whole time. But her trust in the Lord and her commitment to fulfill her calling never faltered, perhaps because she knew of the truth contained in her name. We have already discovered that her name means "Jehovah has sworn," but the root word of the second part of her name comes from the Hebrew word for *seven*, the number of completion, and means "to seven oneself, i.e. swear (as if repeating a declaration seven times)."[6] I wonder if every time Joash reached another birthday, Jehosheba rejoiced at the fact that the Lord was keeping the seed of David on the throne, as He had sworn to do—and then realized when Joash reached his seventh birthday that her assignment was complete.

A mark of distinction in the legendary woman is a finisher's mentality. Jesus boldly proclaimed, "My food is to do the will of Him who sent Me, and to finish His work" (John 4:34). The legendary woman is prepared to see her assignment through to completion, whether it takes seven minutes, seven years, or seven decades. She will not let hardness of heart hinder her. She has the Spirit of God within her so she can walk in righteousness and keep her heart soft and open to the Lord's leading.

Your Defining Moment

Are you ready for your defining moment, when you will have to take courage and forge ahead in the face of fear to fulfill your calling? Remember, courage is developed by your everyday choices. Your defining moment of courage may come tomorrow, next week, next month, next year, or even years from now, but you need to prepare your heart for it today.

Bethany Hamilton's defining moment came when she chose to get back in the water and surf again after losing her arm in a shark attack. She wrote:

> Being courageous isn't about pretending that bad things don't happen or that real risks are all in our head. Being courageous is being honest with what we are facing and feeling then pushing on. We are fueled by our preparation and we can take a risk in pursuit of a goal. The good news is that we can practice courage every day.[7]

Rosa Parks' defining moment came when she chose to not give up her seat on a bus. But she had been preparing her heart long before that moment:

> As a child, I learned from the Bible to trust in God and not be afraid....I saw and heard so much as a child growing up with hate and injustice against black people. I learned to put my trust in God and to seek Him as my strength. Long ago I set my mind to be a free person and not to give in to fear....I have learned over the years that when one's mind is made up, this diminished fear; knowing what must be done does away with fear.[8]

And Rosa's preparation paid off. By making the decision to do what was right over and over again, she was deciding not to let her heart be hardened. The choices she made on a daily basis, even though she regularly faced racism, Jim Crow laws, disrespect, mistreatment, and oppression, developed the courage she needed for that moment on a bus in Montgomery, Alabama, in 1955. "I did not feel any fear," she wrote. "I felt the Lord would give me the strength to endure whatever I had to face. God did away with all my fear. It was time for someone to stand up—or in my case, sit down. I refused to move."[9]

Your defining moment could be any number of things. You may face physical peril or a devastating diagnosis. God may call upon you to stand for justice or fight for truth in a time when justice and truth are hard to come by. Your assignment may be to fulfill the Great Commission and go into the unknown on a mission of mercy. You may suffer for righteousness' sake. But no matter your moment, you are not alone. God is with you. He sees you. He is on your side. And "with God all things are possible" (Matt. 19:26). With God's protection and guidance you should be able to conquer your fears and live a life full of determination. It is God who commands you to have courage, for that means having faith and confidence in Him.

Legendary women such as Jehosheba, Bethany Hamilton, and Rosa Parks have given us the gift of a legacy of courage. It is time to not let shame, rejection, feelings of inadequacy or inferiority, insecurity, passivity, or fear stand in your way. It is time to take courage! It's time to take hold of the promises of God so you can let go of the fear. God's Word is full of promises that you can stand on each and every day and when you reach your defining moment.

> For God has not given us a spirit of fear, but of power and of love and of a sound mind.
> —2 Timothy 1:7

> Fear not, for I am with you; be not dismayed, for I am your God. I will strengthen you, yes, I will help you, I will uphold you with My righteous right hand.
> —Isaiah 41:10

Fear not, for I have redeemed you; I have called you by
your name; you are Mine.

—ISAIAH 43:1

The LORD is on my side; I will not fear.

—PSALM 118:6

Fear is the greatest enemy of the call of God. Fear always
binds and blocks movement and advancement. Braveheart, it
is time to arise and act and see God's will prevail. Prepare
your heart, and take courage. God is releasing courage to take
action and learn as you go. These are the days when the Lord
is releasing grace and courage to break up and break through
blockages and restrictions to your obedience. God is releasing
and opening the floodgates of favor and faith to empower you
to fulfill your destiny.

PRAYER FOR AWAKENING YOUR BRAVE HEART

*Father, Your Word admonishes me to be of good courage,
and You will strengthen my heart (Ps. 31:24; Deut.
31:6). I ask that You will awaken courage within my
heart to do Your will. Give me boldness to initiate Your
assignment and courage to endure to completion. Father,
give me the courage and strength to seize every opportunity You have placed in my path to fulfill my assignment
in the earth. I pray that You will strengthen my heart to
be brave. Create in me a brave heart!*

*Lord, I ask that You remove the hardened heart, the
stony heart, the broken heart, the angry heart, and
replace it with a tender heart. Create in me a lionlike
heart. I want to boldly speak Your truth with passion.
Let the words of my mouth and the meditations of my
heart be acceptable in Your sight. I want to bravely stand
for justice. I want to bravely stand for what I believe.*

Lord, Your Word says that out of the abundance of the heart the mouth speaks. Let my heart be filled with courage and bravery. Let me be led by my convictions and not my fears. Lord, I ask that You release the courage and grit to push through difficult plateaus in my life. Lord, whatever challenges or difficulties I might face, I choose to walk bravely through them with Your help. I will not sit on the sidelines of life and fearfully watch others fulfill their destiny.

DECLARATIONS AGAINST THE ENEMIES OF COURAGE AND THE BRAVE HEART

I declare I will leave a legacy of courage!

I will not allow fear to stop me from advancing in the purposes of God for my life.

I declare that the perfect love of God casts out all fear.

I declare that God is always with me! He will not forsake me in my assignment.

God is a good Father, and He will never abandon me.

I choose to stand for righteousness in the midst of social disapproval.

I will persevere in the face of danger by the power of the Holy Spirit.

I suppress every desire to give up and play it safe! I will not settle for safe. I loose myself from halfway, almost, and just enough!

I am a risk taker.

I am a history maker.

I will challenge the status quo.

I will move at a moment's notice to rescue the downtrodden and oppressed.

I will break myself and everyone connected to me out of the box of limitations.

I break stagnation and passivity off my life.

I will not live in shame or fear of failure.

I will not be intimidated by past mistakes or moral failure. I am a new creature in Christ.

I am not inadequate. I can do all things through Christ who strengthens me.

I will not be intimidated. I loose myself from all voices of failure and defeat!

I will arise with a brave heart and take action to see God's will prevail in the earth!

Chapter 3

LEADING WITH LOVE

*Legendary Women Are Fiercely Loving and
Driven by Compassion*

Compassion is the greatest form of
love humans have to offer.

—Rachel Scott

T HE LEGENDARY WOMAN possesses a fierce love for others and is driven by compassion. Her heart is not only soft and strong, but it is also full. Because of the love that has been shown to her by her heavenly Father, she can't help but want to love others. She loves the Lord with all her heart, soul, mind, and strength, and she loves her neighbor as herself (Mark 12:30–31). She knows that her love for others marks her as a disciple of Jesus (John 13:35). She also recognizes that keeping God's commandments is how she abides in His love (John 15:10).

The legendary woman even has a heart to love her enemies and those who are considered unlovely. She knows Jesus meant it when He said, "Inasmuch as you did it to one of the least of these My brethren, you did it to Me" (Matt. 25:40). While the legendary woman of course loves her family and friends, she also possesses a fierce love for people whom the world would not expect her to love. She is not afraid to cross social and cultural boundaries to demonstrate the love and compassion imparted to her by the Lord.

The dictionary defines *love* as "strong affection for another arising out of kinship or personal ties,"[1] but the biblical definition goes far beyond that. Beyond loving the Lord and our families and friends, the Bible tells us to love our neighbors (Lev. 19:18), our enemies (Matt. 5:44), and the stranger (Deut. 10:19). It also tells us that love is more than just a feeling; love involves action.

> Love suffers long and is kind; love does not envy; love does not parade itself, is not puffed up; does not behave rudely, does not seek its own, is not provoked, thinks no evil; does not rejoice in iniquity, but rejoices in the truth; bears all things, believes all things, hopes all things, endures all things. Love never fails.
> —1 CORINTHIANS 13:4–8

> Through love serve one another.
> —GALATIANS 5:13

Compassion is defined as "sympathetic consciousness of others' distress together with a desire to alleviate it."[2] The Greek word translated "compassion" in the New Testament in verses such as Matthew 9:36 and 14:14, which speak of Jesus' compassion for the multitudes that followed Him, means to have sympathy and to be moved with compassion.[3] It speaks of sympathy that stirs you to action. And this is the heart of the legendary woman. She doesn't just feel love and compassion. She doesn't just have a desire to alleviate the distress of others. She takes action. She does something about it. She will not let hatred, apathy, complacence, or hardness of heart hinder her. The legendary woman is never content to sit back and do nothing when love and compassion move her heart; when her heart is moved, she moves.

CHOOSING LOVE

Our biblical legendary woman who demonstrated this fierce love and driving compassion is the daughter of Pharaoh. She grew up with the proverbial silver spoon in her mouth, but she wasn't selfish, prideful, and arrogant, as one might expect. She lived in a time of great fear and prejudice. The children of Israel had relocated to Egypt because of a famine. When first in Egypt, the Israelites enjoyed a secure position since Joseph, the son of Jacob, was second in command over the land, and they "were fruitful and increased abundantly, multiplied and grew exceedingly mighty; and the land was filled with them" (Exod. 1:7).

But then a generation or two passed, and Egypt got a new king, one who didn't know Joseph.

> And he said to his people, "Look, the people of the children of Israel are more and mightier than we; come, let us deal shrewdly with them, lest they multiply, and it happen, in the event of war, that they also join our enemies and fight against us, and so go up out of the land." Therefore they set taskmasters over them to afflict them with their burdens....But the more they afflicted them, the more they multiplied and grew. And they were in dread of the children of Israel.
>
> —Exodus 1:9–12

Out of fear Pharaoh devised a plan to have the Hebrew midwives kill any baby boys born to the children of Israel. But the midwives, Shiphrah and Puah—legendary women in their own right because of their great courage—refused to cooperate. So Pharaoh issued a command:

> Every son who is born you shall cast into the river, and every daughter you shall save alive.
>
> —Exodus 1:22

It is in the midst of these circumstances that we meet Pharaoh's daughter. The children of Israel have been oppressed and enslaved. The Egyptians are acting with great prejudice and cruelty out of fear. And one courageous and loving mother, in an attempt to save her infant son from the death ordered by Pharaoh, makes an ark for him. She places her son and her hope in an ark of bulrushes and lays it in the reeds by the riverbank.

> Then the daughter of Pharaoh came down to bathe at the river. And her maidens walked along the riverside; and when she saw the ark among the reeds, she sent her maid to get it. And when she opened it, she saw the child, and behold, the baby wept. So she had compassion on him, and said, "This is one of the Hebrews' children."
>
> Then his sister said to Pharaoh's daughter, "Shall I go and call a nurse for you from the Hebrew women, that she may nurse the child for you?"
>
> And Pharaoh's daughter said to her, "Go." So the maiden went and called the child's mother. Then Pharaoh's daughter said to her, "Take this child away and nurse him for me, and I will give you your wages." So the woman took the child and nursed him. And the child grew, and she brought him to Pharaoh's daughter, and he became her son. So she called his name Moses, saying, "Because I drew him out of the water."
>
> —EXODUS 2:5–10

Pharaoh's daughter had likely been conditioned to fear and perhaps even hate the children of Israel. Maybe you have faced a similar situation. There may be other cultures or races or social groups that you have been conditioned to fear or even hate. But as a legendary woman, you must choose to see beyond the labels. The Word says that "there is neither Jew nor Greek, there is neither slave nor free, there is neither male nor female; for you are all one in Christ Jesus" (Gal. 3:28). We are all one in Christ Jesus, so the legendary woman will not let social or cultural barriers stand in her way. She will choose love. I believe this act of fierce love is going to be required to heal the racial divide in America! Legendary women must actively find ways to cross racial barriers embedded in our world systems.

When Pharaoh's daughter reached her defining moment, when she discovered a baby boy in an ark of bulrushes in the river, she laid aside her prejudices. She chose action over apathy. She chose to show love and compassion, at great risk to herself. She adopted a son of the people her father sought to kill, broke the law of the land, and risked her own reputation, crown, and personal safety to essentially become a female savior for the children of Israel. Hearing the cries of the enslaved child, Moses, she answered them with enormous faith, compassion, and love. I want to make a declaration right now over your life, that the Holy Spirit will sensitize your heart to the cries of this generation. As it did with Jesus, let compassion move you to bring relief to the disenfranchised in your nation. Let compassion drive you to do something! I decree an awakening in your heart.

I'm sure Pharaoh's daughter had no inclination of who the baby boy she rescued would grow up to be. She didn't know that Moses would lead the children of Israel out of Egypt under the miraculous hand of the Lord God Almighty. She didn't know he would lift up his rod and watch the Red Sea peel back in a supernatural rescue of epic proportions. She didn't know that the Lord would talk to Moses "face to face, as a man speaks to his friend" (Exod. 33:11). She didn't know that the Lord would give the Law to the children of Israel through Moses. What she did know was that she had an opportunity to do the right thing, to show mercy and compassion, and to save the life of one baby boy. Her actions were legendary!

When you, legendary woman, have an opportunity to do the right thing, to show love and compassion, you will often have no idea what the long-term outcome will be. But you will still act, because the size of the impact of your actions doesn't really matter. When the Lord moves your heart with compassion, you will move. You won't let hate hinder you. You will be faithful to the calling God has placed on your life. You will love because He first loved you. You will pour out compassion because of the compassion poured out on you. I believe the Lord is calling every woman reading this book to take the risks necessary to secure lineages, legacies, whole cultures, and generations of people. God wants you to be the answer to questions such as "If I don't save this one...if I do not clothe or feed this one...if I do not love this one, who will?"

Pharaoh's daughter went beyond just saving Moses' life. She adopted him as her son, and there is no more profound picture of love. She chose to love him. She chose him to be part of her family. She chose to spend years of her life raising him to be a man. She chose him, just as God chose you:

> [In His love] He chose us in Christ [actually selected us for Himself as His own] before the foundation of the world, so that we would be holy [that is, consecrated, set apart for Him, purpose-driven] and blameless in His sight. In love He predestined and lovingly planned for us to be adopted to Himself as [His own] children through Jesus Christ, in accordance with the kind intention and good pleasure of His will.
>
> —EPHESIANS 1:4–5, AMP

When you choose to love someone, especially someone others might consider unlovable, it is a reflection of God's love in you. It puts hands and feet on the love of God so that it can reach the lost. The love and compassion of the legendary woman is God's love in action.

There is a saying in the Talmud that anyone who saves the life of one Jewish person saves the whole world.[4] And Pharaoh's daughter's choice in her defining moment displayed the truth of that statement. While Moses was from the tribe of Levi, the tribe of Judah—from which Jesus descended—was one of the tribes Moses led out of Egyptian captivity. Pharaoh's daughter's compassion spared one baby boy, and because of that, another baby boy was eventually born into this world to die on a cross to spare any who would believe in Him.

The Hebrew word translated "compassion" in Exodus 2:6 also means to spare.[5] Little did Pharaoh's daughter know that by sparing one life, billions more would eventually be spared. Love is a powerful force, and in our self-absorbed society it gets little recognition. God is love, and He is highlighting the importance of being a living flame of love to the world. Legendary woman, God places great value on our learning to love others and demonstrating that love through action.

And keep in mind that Pharaoh's daughter put herself at risk by disobeying Pharaoh and adopting a Hebrew boy. Moses was circumcised when he was eight days old, so anyone who changed him or gave him a bath would know the truth of his origin. But the legendary woman is willing to take risks to love those whom she has been called to love because her love is backed by courage and driven by compassion.

THE LEAST OF THESE

Another legendary woman known for her fierce love and driving compassion was Mother Teresa of Calcutta. A Catholic nun, she originally taught in a high school for girls. But then she experienced what has been termed a "call within a call" that changed the trajectory of her life—it was her defining moment. She said the Lord spoke to her and told her to go work in the slums of Calcutta with the city's poor, sick, and destitute. In 1950, with only a handful of others, she founded the Missionaries of Charity, which established an orphanage, a nursing home, a leper colony, mobile health clinics, and other charitable works in Calcutta and then around the world. By the time of her death the Missionaries of Charity had 610 foundations in 123 different countries.[6]

Mother Teresa understood what Jesus meant about loving

"the least of these" (Matt. 25:40). When asked how to overcome fear in a situation such as having to touch a person with leprosy, Mother Teresa said:

> If you really love that person then it will be easier for you to accept that person and it will be with love and kindness. For that is an opportunity for you to put your love for God in living action. For love begins at home. And for us in our Scriptures it is very clearly said. What Jesus said was, "Whatever you do to the least of my brethren, you do it to me."[7]

Mother Teresa's love and compassion made her a legend in her own time. She sacrificed whatever was necessary to fulfill the calling of God on her life to love others. She said, "I felt God wanted something more from me. He wanted me to...love Him in the distressing disguise of the poorest of the poor."[8]

That is what legendary women do. They love others selflessly because of the love God has shown them. They are driven by compassion to be the hands and feet of Jesus on the earth. They won't let any kind of barrier—be it physical, emotional, financial, social, cultural, or any other kind—get in the way of their calling to love others. By the power of the Holy Spirit, they embody the biblical definition of *love*.

Seventeen-year-old Rachel Scott, the first victim in the Columbine school shooting, understood that. She understood the power of love and compassion. I believe her defining moment came when she decided that she was going to live wholeheartedly for Jesus, no matter the cost. She recognized that she would lose friends over it; her journals imply that she even knew she would lose her life over it. But she still committed to being the hands and feet of Jesus to those God put in her path. She especially wanted to reach out to those who were marginalized or overlooked by others, including people with special needs, new students, and those who were being bullied or picked on.[9] And Rachel didn't just write about these things. She took action. At Rachel's funeral, one young man sobbed and said, "All my life I prayed that someone would love me and make me feel wanted. God sent me an angel."[10]

In an essay, Rachel wrote, "Compassion is the greatest form of love humans have to offer....I have this theory that if one person can go out of their way to show compassion, then it will start a chain reaction of the same. People will never know how far a little kindness can go."[11] And Rachel's theory was correct. Her acts of kindness started a chain reaction, inspiring others, decreasing violence and bullying in schools, and increasing kindness and compassion.[12] When she was thirteen years old, Rachel traced her hands on the back of her dresser and wrote, "These hands belong to Rachel Joy Scott and will someday touch millions of people's hearts."[13] Her prophecy was fulfilled. Even though her life was tragically cut short, her love and compassion were a legacy that touched millions.

The love of a legendary woman is fierce. It is tenacious. It is strong. It is a driving force that allows the legendary woman to walk in the fullness of her calling. And her love and compassion motivate her to leave a legacy of love behind her, knowing that legacy of fierce love and driving compassion will be passed down from generation to generation of legendary women.

YOUR DEFINING MOMENT

Pharaoh's daughter chose a name for the baby boy she rescued from the river. She named him Moses, which means drawn or drawing out.[14] And drawing out is what love often looks like—drawing someone out of danger, out of loneliness, out of bondage, out of hopelessness, out of despair. Pharaoh's daughter drew Moses out of danger. Mother Teresa drew people out of loneliness and hopelessness. Rachel Scott drew people out of feeling invisible, unwanted, and unloved. What will you draw someone out of? What will your defining moment of fierce love and driving compassion look like?

You could be endowed with supernatural strength in your fierce-love defining moment, like Lydia Angyiou, who went head to head with a polar bear to protect her seven-year-old son, or like Lauren Kornacki, who lifted a BMW off her father after a jack slipped.[15] Maybe your defining moment will be when your heart is captivated by a little girl with special needs and you choose to make her part of your family through adoption. Your moment could occur when you finally step out to start a ministry to the hungry, the hurting, or the hopeless. Your moment could occur when you train young girls in how to start their own businesses. Your moment might be when your prodigal son or daughter finally comes home after you prayed tenaciously for years, going boldly before the throne of grace over and over again out of love for your child.

The Syro-Phoenician woman mentioned in the Gospel of Mark is an example of a legendary woman who didn't give up. She loved her daughter so much that "she kept asking [Jesus] to cast the demon out of her daughter" (7:26). The verb translated "kept asking" means to ask, beg, beseech, or entreat, and the tense means that she did it over and over again.[16] She knew that Jesus was the only hope for her daughter, and her love for her daughter meant that she was not going to give up until Jesus set her free.

That is the kind of love a legendary woman has—a love that never gives up. God is giving you the capacity to recognize that the world offers many kinds of love that are only a shadow of the real thing. There is a new wisdom to know that the world offers comfort through indulgence, food, lust, entertainment, and countless other methods, but that kind of comfort is only temporary. The legendary woman knows the Holy Spirit is the real Comforter, the One who can offer comfort that lasts forever, regardless of circumstances. And because of her love and compassion, the legendary woman wants others to know the Comforter the way she does. And she knows the love of God operating in and through her will draw people to the God of all comfort, the God who is love.

Jesus said, "Greater love has no one than this, than to lay down one's life for his friends" (John 15:13). When we hear this verse, we often think about dying to save someone. And there have been times when legendary women have done exactly that—they have died to save others—such as Sandy Hook teacher Victoria Soto, who died trying to shield her students from a gunman. But what about when laying down your life is about dying to yourself? The legendary woman understands that Jesus' words were about so much more than physical death. She understands that great love, fierce love, often requires sacrifice, requires dying to herself.

Legendary woman Florence Nightingale understood this. She left behind a life of wealth and privilege to pursue what she knew was her divine purpose. She laid down her life. It wasn't always easy, but she knew what God had called her to do. During a time of struggle, she wrote:

> I must do without some things—as many as I can—which I could not have without causing more suffering than I am obliged to cause any way....Father, not my will but thine be done. Father of Truth, of Wisdom, of Goodness....I have been brought hither by the laws of God....I shall be brought through by the laws of God.[17]

Nightingale sacrificed the comfortable and familiar to become a nurse, and the end result saved more lives than most of us could even fathom, whether directly through her care or indirectly through the nursing standards and health-care reforms she championed. She was a legendary woman of fierce love and driving compassion.

Legendary woman, it is time to rise up and love the people

around you the way God has called you to. It is time to take hold of the legacy of love left for you by countless other legendary women who have loved fiercely and build a legacy of your own. Start with the basics.

> Love the LORD your God with all your heart, with all your soul, and with all your strength.
>
> —DEUTERONOMY 6:5

> Love your neighbor as yourself.
>
> —LEVITICUS 19:18

> A new commandment I give to you, that you love one another; as I have loved you, that you also love one another.
>
> —JOHN 13:34

Legendary woman, because of the Holy Spirit working in and through you, your love, kindness, and compassion can break through barriers, tear down walls, move mountains, heal wounds, comfort the lonely, and give hope to the hopeless. It is time to give good news to the poor, heal the brokenhearted, proclaim liberty to the captives, open the prison of those who are bound, comfort those who mourn, and give them beauty for ashes and the garment of praise for the spirit of heaviness (Isa. 61:1–3). It is time to draw people out of bondage, danger, and despair.

PRAYER TO AWAKEN FIERCE LOVE

Father, set Your seal of love upon my heart (Song of Sol. 8:6–7). *I ask that You will awaken Your vehement flames of love in me. Holy Spirit, teach me how to love and serve humanity purely from Your eternal love. Lavish me with Your great love that I may lavishly love others* (1 John 3:1).

Father, I ask that You will cause Your fierce love for me to fill my heart. I want to know the length, the depth, and the height of the eternal love of the heavenly Father, bestowed upon me because I am called Your daughter. Burn Your love into my heart. Let Your unfailing love saturate and permeate my very being until it overflows, until it spills out in every area of my life. Let Your fierce love escort me through every obstacle and battle I face! Father, let me experience the heights and depths of Your love.

DECLARATIONS AGAINST THE ENEMIES OF LOVE

I am a legendary lover of God.

I will release God's love wherever He leads me.

I loose myself from hurt and pain.

I loose myself from bound and blocked emotions.

I will love my neighbor as myself.

I will not operate in cold love.

I will not allow past hurts, pains, and betrayals to create a stumbling block to compassion.

I loose myself from all hatred.

I loose myself from any form of racial prejudice.

Lord, break me free from idolatry of skin.

I decree that compassion is love in action.

Let true compassion arise in my very being.

Let compassion cause me to love humanity and motivate me to relieve their pain.

Chapter 4

THE NEW NORMAL

Legendary Women Are Obedient to God

Obedience to God is the pathway to the life you really
want to live. It's the answer to overcoming sin and any
problem you face. It's the way we learn how to grow up
and let God work in our lives, gently changing us so
we can be what He created us to be.

—Joyce Meyer

O BEDIENCE TO GOD is the pathway to life, as Joyce
Meyer wrote. And I believe God is redeeming and
restoring the essence of this character trait in our day.
Women have been told to sit down, be quiet, and obey what
others say for centuries, but legendary women are arising to
model true obedience. The major fruit of obedience is that you
will eat the good of the land.

Words such as *obedience* and *submission* often have negative connotations in today's world because of people who have
abused their authority in the past. The words may bring to mind
images of obedient people being prisoners to the authority over
them. But the truth is that there is great freedom in obeying
the Lord and submitting to His will for your life. He does not
abuse His authority. His intention is not to keep you imprisoned, bound in shackles of dos and don'ts. In fact the Lord is
calling to you, saying:

> Awake, awake! Put on your strength....Shake yourself
> from the dust, arise....Loose yourself from the bonds of
> your neck, O captive daughter of Zion!
> —Isaiah 52:1–2

When you are stuck in sin, you are a prisoner. The Scripture asks:

> Do you not know that to whom you present yourselves slaves to obey, you are that one's slaves whom you obey, whether of sin leading to death, or of obedience leading to righteousness?
>
> —ROMANS 6:16

You are either a slave to sin or a slave to righteousness. The world may try to tell you that there is freedom in doing whatever you want, but there is always a price to pay for going against God. It may not always be obvious, but at the very least it hardens your heart, something the Word warns against time and again (e.g., Ps. 95:8; Prov. 28:14). It grieves the heart of God when people harden their hearts (Mark 3:5). Disobedience is rebellion, and that is something God takes very seriously. In fact He said rebellion is "as the sin of witchcraft":

> For rebellion is as the sin of witchcraft, and stubbornness is as iniquity and idolatry.
>
> —1 SAMUEL 15:23

In today's society many view rebelling against authority as a good thing. Rebels are upheld as heroic and brave. And while there is a place for rebelling against things that oppose the Word of God, there is no place for the legendary woman to rebel just for the sake of rebellion. The Word of God makes this clear:

> Let every soul be subject to the governing authorities. For there is no authority except from God, and the authorities that exist are appointed by God. Therefore whoever resists the authority resists the ordinance of God, and those who resist will bring judgment on themselves.
>
> —ROMANS 13:1–2

That means unless an authority is telling you to do something contrary to the Word of God, you are called to submit and obey—because ultimately you are submitting to and obeying God. I have found that the ways of the Lord are not grievous. Submitting to the authority over my life provides protection and safety. There is a great freedom in obeying the Lord, and He wants you to be free. He wants you to walk in freedom, walk in obedience, walk in submission to His will. He paid a great price for your freedom, but it's up to you to choose to walk in it.

Don't be hindered by a rebellious spirit. The Spirit of the Lord is declaring that now is the time for you to "stand fast… in the liberty by which Christ has made [you] free, and do not be entangled again with a yoke of bondage" (Gal. 5:1). There is an assignment of the enemy to get women in a place of rebellion and bondage. This could also expose you to a spirit of witchcraft. We must discern the tactics of the enemy.

OBEDIENCE UNTO DEATH

Jesus' death on the cross was itself an act of obedience:

> And being found in fashion as a man, he humbled himself, and became obedient unto death, even the death of the cross.
>
> —PHILIPPIANS 2:8, KJV

There have been, there are, and there will be legendary women obedient unto physical death, and theirs is an amazing legacy of faith, obedience, and courage. But as I mentioned before, death isn't always about physically dying; sometimes it is about dying to yourself. It is about laying down your life for the high calling of God in Christ Jesus. It is about laying your plans and your desires at the feet of Jesus and saying, "Not my will but Yours be done." It is about telling God, "I want

Your plans and Your desires for my life." God is faithful. You can trust Him, knowing that His plans for you are for good, to give you hope and a future (Jer. 29:11), and that when you delight yourself in Him, He will give you the desires of your heart (Ps. 37:4).

Like her Son Jesus, Mary modeled a level of obedience that has made her a central topic of discussion among philosophers, theologians, and laypeople for millennia. Put yourself in Mary's shoes. You're a teenager, engaged to be married to a carpenter named Joseph. An angel comes to you and tells you that you are going to get pregnant and have a Son, who "will be great, and will be called the Son of the Highest; and the Lord God will give Him the throne of His father David. And He will reign over the house of Jacob forever, and of His kingdom there will be no end" (Luke 1:32–33; see also vv. 26–31). You naturally have questions about how exactly that is going to happen since you are a virgin. The angel explains how this will be, tells you that your barren relative Elizabeth is also pregnant, and says, "For with God nothing will be impossible" (Luke 1:37; see also vv. 34–36).

Instead of fighting God or telling Him she wasn't the right person for the job, Mary chose obedience. She chose to live out God's purpose for her life, even though she didn't know where it would lead. I want to bring this scenario into the twenty-first century. If you are reading this book and maybe contemplating an abortion, your decision to keep the child is legendary. God will provide for you and the baby. You could be carrying the next president, an inventor, or the greatest preacher of the gospel to be born. Don't allow fear or shame to push you into doing something you may regret later. I release courage and faith into your heart to make the right decision.

I imagine Mary probably had no idea what the results of her obedience would be—giving birth in a stable; angels and shepherds and wise men, and a wicked king forcing them to flee to a foreign country; raising the Messiah, along with the other children she had later; watching her Son teach the Word, turn water into wine, heal the sick, and raise the dead; witnessing her Son's brutal crucifixion; rejoicing at Jesus' resurrection and triumph over death, hell, and the grave; and the coming of the Holy Spirit—but she chose to obey, even when facing the unknown. Her obedience had a price—Simeon prophesied that a sword would pierce Mary's soul, and indeed it did when she watched Jesus hanging on a cross (Luke 2:35)—but it was a price she willingly paid.

Eerdmans Dictionary of the Bible states that "if one truly hears the word of God, then obedience is inevitable. Thus, if people fail to obey, the prophets often accuse the Israelites of being deaf." Pointing to Eerdmans' definition of *obedience*, blogger Mary Fairchild wrote, "True 'hearing,' or obedience, involves the physical hearing that inspires the hearer, and a belief or trust that in turn motivates the hearer to act in accordance with the speaker's desires."[1] The legendary woman is one who hears from the Lord and then acts in obedience out of her trust in the Lord. We must learn to submit our wills to the will of the Lord. Mary heard an instruction from the Lord that transcended her natural understanding and abilities, but she totally submitted to the authority of God.

And while Mary clearly left a legacy of obedience for those who came after her, she also passed on the lesson of obedience during her lifetime. For example, when she was at a wedding in Cana and they ran out of wine, she told Jesus what the problem was. She then told the servants, "Whatever He says to you, do it" (John 2:5; see also vv. 1–4). The servants obeyed, and because of their obedience, even when what they were being told to do made no sense, they witnessed a miracle. Jesus told them to fill some pots with water, draw some out, and bring it to the master of the feast. It made no sense in the eyes of the world to bring a cup of water to a man who was expecting wine. But the servants obeyed and found that they had served excellent wine to the master. Obedience resulted in a miracle, and obedience can result in miracles in your life too. When God calls you to do something, trust Him and do it. You are a legendary woman of fiery faith and great courage, and the Holy Spirit is empowering you to be obedient for the glory of the Lord.

Legendary women are still exhibiting devoted obedience today. In September 2001, Sun Minghua was arrested in China "on suspicion of organizing and utilizing a cult organization to undermine law enforcement." The arrest was related to her involvement with the South China Church, an underground church with approximately one hundred thousand members. Two years after getting saved, Minghua had "devoted herself to preaching the gospel." She knew the risks involved—that she could be imprisoned or even executed—but she obeyed the call of the Lord on her life, eventually becoming a council member in charge of finances for the underground church. But this legendary woman was obedient to the Lord. After her arrest she was initially sentenced to life in prison, but her sentence was reduced.[2] She still spent ten years in jail, where she was denied access to medical care and was forbidden to read the Bible or pray. Her requests to pray or read the Bible were met with threats of losing family visitation privileges. While she was still imprisoned, her sister reported that the spiritual pain she endured from not being able to read the Bible was more painful than physical torture.[3]

Asia Bibi, a Pakistani woman, was arrested in 2009. She was sentenced to death under Pakistan's blasphemy law. Her crime was simply sharing the gospel with the women she worked with when they had a discussion about faith. Asia knew the risks. She was aware of the blasphemy law and the penalty it carried. Yet she chose to share the gospel and be obedient. She took to heart what the Word says:

> But sanctify the Lord God in your hearts, and always be ready to give a defense to everyone who asks you a reason for the hope that is in you, with meekness and fear; having a good conscience, that when they defame you as evildoers, those who revile your good conduct in Christ may be ashamed.
>
> —1 PETER 3:15–16

Asia's case went all the way to the Supreme Court of Pakistan, and the public outcry about her sentence continued during the entire process. Literally tens of thousands of letters and emails were sent on her behalf, requesting her release. She was eventually acquitted and released after spending over nine years in prison.[4]

Both Minghua and Asia chose to obey the Lord. They chose to trust. And even though their obedience had a price, just as it did with Mary, it was a price they gladly paid. Obedience isn't always easy. In fact it is often hard. You may find yourself wondering if you have the strength to obey, but remember that when you are weak, you are strong, for God's strength is made perfect in your weakness (2 Cor. 12:9–10). When you are unhindered by rebellion, when you have the heart to obey, when you want God's will more than your own, God will empower you to walk in obedience to His will.

WALKING IN FREEDOM

Your heavenly Father wants you to be free. He wants it so much that He sent His Son to die on a cross "to proclaim liberty to the captives, and the opening of the prison to those who are bound" (Isa. 61:1). So it's time to wake up, shake off the shackles of sin, arise, and walk in the freedom that Christ died to give you.

As followers of Christ, we are called to obedience. The Word says:

> Has the LORD as great delight in burnt offerings and sacrifices, as in obeying the voice of the LORD? Behold, to obey is better than sacrifice, and to heed than the fat of rams.
>
> —1 SAMUEL 15:22

> If you love Me, keep My commandments.
>
> —JOHN 14:15

The Word also lets us know that there are great benefits to obedience:

> If you are willing and obedient, you shall eat the good of the land.
>
> —ISAIAH 1:19

> Jesus answered and said to him, "If anyone loves Me, he will keep My word; and My Father will love him, and We will come to him and make Our home with him."
>
> —JOHN 14:23

Obedience is an act of worship. There is no better way to show the Lord that you love and trust Him than by obeying Him. And obedience starts with addressing the sin issues in your life. Legendary woman, when you recognize you are on the wrong path, the sooner you repent and get back on the right path, the better. As I have said before, the wrong road does not become the right road until you turn around and go back to where you were before you took the wrong turn.

The legendary woman is called to a life of obedience. Going beyond trying not to sin, the legendary woman steps out in faith to do whatever the Lord is calling her to do, even when it makes no sense in the eyes of the world or even in her own eyes. The legendary woman is the one who will sell everything to go to the mission field to reach the lost, move to another state or even another country at the drop of a hat just because the Lord said go, or give up an extremely lucrative career to go into full-time ministry because she knows it is her divine calling, her divine purpose.

YOUR DEFINING MOMENT

Mary, Minghua, and Asia all had defining moments—moments when they chose to obey the Lord despite the substantial risks to their lives. Each of those legendary women made the choice to risk her physical life. And your defining moment may pose that choice. Will you risk dying to fulfill the purpose and plan that God has for you?

Yet it is more likely that your defining moment of obedience will be when you have to decide if you are willing to die to yourself. Dying to self is dying to selfish ambition. Obedience becomes a battle of wills. It's a process of hearing and obeying the commandments of the Lord. It's discerning His will and embracing it, even though it may be painful to the flesh and scary to the human mind.

But the legendary woman accepts the call to obedience. The Holy Spirit will allow her to see life from an eternal realm and give her the wisdom to count the cost. The legendary woman knows that dying to herself is not easy, but she knows that she "can do all things through Christ who strengthens [her]" (Phil. 4:13). She is ready to step out in faith, to do things that make no sense in the eyes of the world, and to run her race with endurance, looking to Jesus, the author and finisher of her faith.

The legendary woman obeys the Word. She listens for and obeys the voice of the Lord. She knows she serves "the faithful God who keeps covenant and mercy for a thousand generations with those who love Him and keep His commandments" (Deut. 7:9). She views her obedience as an act of worship of the God who loves her, redeemed her, and calls her by name. She obeys out of love. The legendary woman isn't imprisoned by her obedience; she knows that her obedience allows her to walk in the liberty that Christ died to give her. She is no longer a captive to sin or hindered by rebellion. She has been set free by the Son, so she is free indeed. The Amplified Bible describes it this way:

> But now since you have been set free from sin and have become [willing] slaves to God, you have your benefit, resulting in sanctification [being made holy and set apart for God's purpose], and the outcome [of this] is eternal life.
>
> —ROMANS 6:22, AMP

I love those words: "set apart for God's purpose." That is what is behind the obedience of the legendary woman. She has been set apart for God's purpose. She has set her heart and her mind to pursue that purpose, and she is not going to let anything stand in her way. She knows she has been chosen. She is part of "a chosen generation, a royal priesthood, a holy nation, His own special people" (1 Pet. 2:9). She is one whom Jesus chose before the foundation of the world that she "should be holy and without blame before Him in love" (Eph. 1:4).

The best way to prepare for your defining moment of obedience is by spending time with the Lord. This is a time of self-examination. It is a time to see your life and purpose from God's perspective. The legendary woman must live life based on God's requirements of her and not society's. Let Him reveal to you the areas of disobedience and rebellion in your life. And keep in mind that delayed obedience is disobedience. When God tells you to act, you need to act.

Spending time with the Lord develops your faith and your trust. You need to encounter the God of your call. When you encounter Him, it gives you fresh focus and perspective. It gives you clarity and determination. An encounter with the Lord of heaven purifies you and equips you to fulfill His plans and purposes for your life. You realize you are exactly who God designed you to be. It gives you confidence so that when God asks, "Who will go?" your answer will be, "Here I am. Send me!" The legendary woman makes time to meet with her King.

Legendary woman, it is time to obey the Lord, no matter what others think and no matter the cost to yourself. It is time to lay your life down at the feet of Jesus and say, "Not my will but Yours be done! I will obey!" It's time to deny yourself, take up your cross, and follow Jesus with all that is in you. It is time for you to leave a legacy of obedience for the generations of legendary women to come. Are you ready?

PRAYER FOR A LIFE OF OBEDIENCE

Lord Jesus, I love You, so I will obey You (John 14:15). To obey You is better than sacrifice (1 Sam. 15:22). I will obey Your Word so that I may eat the good of the land (Isa. 1:19). Holy Spirit, I ask You to reveal any areas of disobedience or rebellion in my life. I repent of my sins and ask You to help me get on the right path and stay there. I will walk with You in freedom, obedience, and submission to Your will. Lord, I pray that not my will but Yours be done in my life. I will delight myself in You so that You will give me the desires of my heart. Let it be to me according to Your word. Equip me to fulfill Your plans and purposes for my life.

DECLARATIONS AGAINST DISOBEDIENCE

I obey the Lord.

I find protection and safety in submitting to authority.

I stand fast in the liberty by which Christ made me free.

I will not be entangled again in the yoke of bondage.

I am not captive to sin.

I am not rebellious.

I am set apart for God's purpose.

I will die to myself.

I want God's plans and desires for my life.

I obey the Lord because I trust Him.

I obey the Lord because I love Him.

I do not delay my obedience.

God's strength is made perfect in my weakness.

I can do all things through Christ, who strengthens me.

I will step out in faith.

I run my race with endurance, looking to Jesus, the author and finisher of my faith.

I listen for and obey the voice of the Lord.

Chapter 5

GOING TOE TO TOE FOR JUSTICE
AND RIGHTEOUSNESS

Legendary Women Know When to Be Confrontational

Confrontation is necessary for growth. If we care,
we will confront and believe God for a favorable
outcome....Only an effective confrontation will bridge
the gap between conflict and cooperation, between
hurt and harmony.

—DEBORAH SMITH PEGUES

WHEN MOST PEOPLE hear the word *confrontational*,
they think of people who are argumentative,
aggressive, arrogant, and antagonistic. But that is
not what I mean when I talk about this character trait. While
the legendary woman is indeed confrontational, it is in the
sense of being a willing advocate for justice and righteousness.

The word *confront* means to have a face-to-face encounter
with someone.[1] It means to oppose something or someone with
firmness or courage.[2] So when I say the legendary woman is
confrontational, I don't mean she is petty or picks arguments
just for the sake of argument or gets in someone's face for no
reason. Instead, the legendary woman is one who can't sit back
and do or say nothing when she sees injustice. She is willing to
take action to make sure that right wins, whether it is for her
sake or for the sake of others. She opposes injustice with the
legendary courage she possesses. She is willing to go head to
head and toe to toe with someone when the need arises. She is
a bold advocate for herself and for others.

The legendary woman also knows the value of maintaining harmony and cooperation in relationships, so she isn't afraid to confront others for the sake of reconciling or maintaining a relationship or to keep a root of bitterness from springing up in her heart. Jesus gave us a clear method for confronting those who have sinned against us. Note that it doesn't include gossiping and complaining to anyone and everyone other than the person who sinned against us. Instead, Jesus said, "If your brother sins against you, go and tell him his fault between you and him alone. If he hears you, you have gained your brother" (Matt. 18:15). Confronting someone in love is a way to restore relationships and make sure bitterness doesn't take root in your heart or in the hearts of others.

But this attribute of the legendary woman is not the one that will win her the Miss Congeniality award. It's more likely to win her a No More Miss Nice Lady award. But this is the character trait that emboldens the legendary woman to raise her voice and take action. She is not going to be silent or still in the face of injustice.

The sixth amendment of the US Constitution has something known as the Confrontation Clause. It means that in a court case, the defendant has the opportunity to face the witnesses, hear their testimony, and dispute that testimony when necessary, the end goal being to arrive at the truth and for justice to be served. And that is the end goal when a legendary woman decides that a confrontation is needed; she wants to make sure truth and justice are upheld. So she will take a seat at the table, call a meeting, step up to the plate, get out the bullhorn, or do whatever else is needed to fulfill her calling as an advocate for herself and others.

OBTAINING THE PROMISE

The daughters of Zelophehad are the biblical legendary women we will look to as an example of being confrontational when the need arises. Zelophehad was of the tribe of Manasseh, and he was one of the children of Israel who died in the wilderness after the exodus from Egypt. Zelophehad had no sons, but he did have five daughters: Mahlah, Noah, Hoglah, Milcah, and Tirzah. When the children of Israel were preparing to finally enter the Promised Land, the Lord told them to take a census of the men who were twenty and older so they could divide up the land as an inheritance. The land was to be divided by lot, with the people inheriting "according to the names of the tribes of their fathers" (Num. 26:55). But since Zelophehad had died without any sons, no one from his family had been numbered in the census.

> Then came the daughters of Zelophehad....And they stood before Moses, before Eleazar the priest, and before the leaders and all the congregation, by the doorway of the tabernacle of meeting, saying: "Our father died in the wilderness; but he was not in the company of those who gathered together against the LORD, in company with Korah, but he died in his own sin; and he had no sons. Why should the name of our father be removed from among his family because he had no son? Give us a possession among our father's brothers."
>
> —NUMBERS 27:1–4

Zelophehad's daughters realized that their father's name was going to be wiped out if they did not receive an inheritance of land among the other members of their tribe. Their request showed great honor to and respect for their father. But their request also showed great faith. Keep in mind that the children of Israel hadn't even entered the Promised Land, and once they entered, they would have to deal with the current inhabitants before the land could be distributed amongst the tribes and families. Though the Promised Land was yet unconquered, the daughters of Zelophehad had full faith in the promises of God.

And they wanted to claim their piece of the promise. As a legendary woman, you need to have full faith in the promises of God and be ready to claim your rightful piece of the promise.

> In Him also we have obtained an inheritance, being predestined according to the purpose of Him who works all things according to the counsel of His will.
>
> —EPHESIANS 1:11

> And we desire that each one of you show the same diligence to the full assurance of hope until the end, that you do not become sluggish, but imitate those who through faith and patience inherit the promises.
>
> —HEBREWS 6:11–12

Zelophehad's daughters believed that having to forfeit their share of the promised inheritance just because they were women was unjust. So they took their case to the highest court in the land—they went before Moses at the doorway to the tabernacle of meeting. It was their defining moment. They didn't spend hours gossiping and whining about their situation. They didn't give up in despair. They didn't try to recruit one of their male cousins to present their case for them. They knew what was right, and they chose to advocate for themselves. They had a face-to-face encounter with Moses and the other leaders of Israel. They had a confrontation, but they presented their case with clarity, stated their demand, and trusted God to do the rest. These were legendary women of great faith and courage who were not afraid to ask for the inheritance that was rightfully theirs.

And the end result was amazing. Moses brought their case before the Lord, which was the right thing to do since His instructions had been to number the men of Israel for dividing up the land. And the Lord responded, "The daughters of Zelophehad speak what is right; you shall surely give them a possession of inheritance among their father's brothers, and cause the inheritance of their father to pass to them" (Num. 27:7). But what was amazing was that the Lord didn't consider His decision to be applicable to Zelophehad's daughters only. It wasn't just a one-time deal. Because of Zelophehad's daughters' willingness to confront the injustice they saw occurring, daughters being allowed to receive their fathers' inheritance if there were no sons became a statute in Israel (vv. 8–11). Their boldness, their faith, and their courage advanced the cause of justice for thousands of women in generation after generation after them. Legendary women are women of vision. Legendary women are women of clarity. Legendary women see the bigger picture. They know that when they fight for truth and justice, it has the potential to impact the generations that will come after them. They will not allow fear and passivity to hinder them.

It's interesting that the names of all five of Zelophehad's daughters carry different shades of the picture of their confrontation and the result. And effective confrontation takes the nature of all five of Zelophehad's daughters working together. While Mahlah literally means disease (poor girl), its root word can mean beseech, intreat, or make supplication.[3] We need to be healed of spiritual disease caused by past hurts before we can effectively confront. We have all been in terrible places and faced horrible things, but the Lord can heal our hearts of injustice so we can effectively fight for justice not in our own strength but with the strength of the Lord. The sisters were beseeching or making supplication to the leaders of Israel for justice. This is the first instance of an appeal for equal rights for women.

Noah means motion, and it comes from a root word that can mean to make move.[4] When the Lord tells us to move, we need to obey and move so that He can prompt others to move. When the sisters were faced with injustice, they didn't just stay still; they went into motion, and the result was God making a move on their behalf.

Milcah means queen but can also be connected to the word *counsel*.[5] When we confront, we need the posture of a queen who carries herself regally with dignity and respect. There are things that need to be confronted and there are things that we just need to let go, and we need the counsel of the Lord to know the difference. Moses sought the counsel of the Lord once the sisters presented their case, and the Lord told Moses that the women were right in their request. The result was that the sisters were granted their own portion of land, their own dominion over which they could be queens.

Tirzah means favorable, and it comes from a root word that means accomplish.[6] We need to pray for favor with God and man so leaders will move on our behalf so that we accomplish what we set out to do.

Hoglah's name means boxer.[7] Her nature was the secret sauce in the formula of confrontation. She was willing to fight because she knew her cause was right. The legendary woman's end goal is to get her leader to hear her voice. I believe as women we have to make sure we are fighting the right cause with the right spirit and the right perspective. Being right in the sight of the Lord is a key factor in confrontation. Confrontation driven by anger or out-of-control emotions is not the way to go.

Because the sisters were willing to be confrontational, to work together, and to advocate for themselves, they received favorable results and accomplished an amazing thing, not only for themselves but also for many other women. The daughters of Zelophehad left a powerful legacy of being confrontational when it comes to advocating for justice. Their willingness to stand up against injustice was responsible not only for a spiritual legacy but also made physical legacies for women possible within the land of Israel. They were legendary women.

YOUR DEFINING MOMENT

There have been many legendary women over the years who have been willing to confront injustice in its many forms, from slavery and racism to human trafficking and inequality. Their defining moments have occurred in courtrooms and board-rooms and barrooms. Whatever the location, these legendary women have accepted the call "to do justly, to love mercy, and to walk humbly with [their] God" (Mic. 6:8). They have been a voice for those who have no voice of their own. They have fought for the cause of justice and righteousness. They boldly stepped forward to be advocates, knowing they carry the power of the Advocate within them (1 John 2:1). They are legendary women, and they have left a legacy of boldness, truth, courage, faith, and power. One such woman was Sojourner Truth.

Born into slavery in New York, Sojourner Truth's original name was Isabella. When New York set a date for emancipation of its slaves, her master told her he would set her free one year before emancipation went into effect if she continued to work hard up until then. But when the time came, he refused to follow through. Sojourner ended up walking away (as opposed to running away, a distinction that was very important to her) from her master and finding employment with some good people. However, her five-year-old son, Peter—who would not be emancipated until he turned twenty-one, according to the law—was illegally sold to a slave owner in Alabama. When Sojourner heard this, she immediately left "to find the man who had thus dared, in the face of all law, human and divine, to sell her child out of the State; and if possible, to bring him to account for the deed."[8]

Eventually the case went to court, and Sojourner won, becoming the first black woman in US history to take a white man to court and win. The man who sold Sojourner's son had to pay a fine, and the Alabama plantation owner was forced to return Peter to his mother. And while I believe the victory in court was a huge moment, I don't believe it was her defining moment of courageous confrontation. I believe that moment occurred when she first set out to find the man who had illegally sold her son. Her first face-to-face encounter was with her former mistress, who treated her with contempt and scorn. But Sojourner was determined; she would have justice, and so would her son. But Sojourner's determination to get her son back caused her former mistress to scorn her even further, asking, "How can you get him? And what have you to support him with, if you could? Have you any money?"[9]

And then Sojourner's defining moment occurred. She knew what was right. She knew what was just. And faith rose up in her like never before. Speaking of that moment, she said, "I know'd I'd have him agin. I was sure God would help me to get him. Why, I felt so *tall within*—I felt as if the *power of a nation* was with me!" So she faced her former mistress and declared slowly, solemnly, and with great determination, "I have no money, but God has enough, or what's better! And I'll have my child again."[10] While many confrontations would follow as she fought to get her son back, I believe Sojourner Truth became the hallmark of the legendary woman who courageously confronts in the cause of justice when her faith blazed like a fire, she declared the truth, and she trusted God with the results.

What will your defining moment of confrontation look like? Will you champion the cause of the oppressed? Will you fight for what is right, even when the world seems to think that what's wrong is not that bad? Will you answer the call to be an advocate for earthly justice? Or for spiritual justice? Will you answer the call to be an advocate for both?

God has placed within each woman the ability to be influential in her circle. Legendary woman, every challenge you face is an entryway to build your strengths or confront your weaknesses. Many times confrontation starts with confronting the woman in the mirror. Confrontation is a tool needed to correct mistakes, measure your success, and define who you are and who you are not.

We live in a time when injustice is rampant. But "the LORD loves justice" (Ps. 37:28). Righteousness and justice are the foundation of His throne (Ps. 89:14). The Book of Isaiah tells us to "learn to do good; seek justice, rebuke the oppressor; defend the fatherless, plead for the widow" (1:17). When we achieve God's justice on the earth, it serves as a light to the nations (Isa. 51:4).

I can't help but think that our innate desire for justice is really about wanting a place to belong, just as Zelophehad's daughters did. We want a place where we are not victims, we are safe, we are not discriminated against, we are free to be ourselves, we are not afraid, we feel loved and accepted, and we can be exactly who God has called us to be. We all want a place to belong, but some people need help finding it, especially when injustice prevails. And that is where the legendary woman comes in.

Legendary woman, God is calling you to be an advocate, to be a voice, to confront. It's time for you to call for "justice [to] run down like water, and righteousness like a mighty stream" (Amos 5:24). It is time for you to claim your rightful spiritual and natural inheritance. Don't let anyone cheat you out of what God has promised you, and don't let anyone cheat others out of the fulfillment of their promises either. It's face-to-face time.

The way you prepare for your defining face-to-face moment is by spending time either face to face with God or facedown in His presence. Spending time in the presence of God changes you. It destroys fear. It destroys passivity. It produces confidence and trust in God. It is where you find fullness of joy (Ps. 16:11). It gives rest (Exod. 33:14). It refreshes (Acts 3:19). And it shakes mountains (Isa. 64:1, 3). You must allow God to develop in you the tenacity, tact, courage, wisdom, and grace you need to accurately present your request. God is raising up women who can be confrontational but also cooperate with authority in order to overcome injustice.

The time to prepare for your defining moment is now. Your moment may come soon, or it may be down the road. But your moment is coming, legendary woman. And just as it was with Zelophehad's daughters, it has the potential to unlock a legacy for countless numbers of women. Are you ready?

PRAYER FOR COURAGE TO CONFRONT INJUSTICE

Lord Jesus, make me a willing advocate for justice and righteousness. Thank You that I have the Advocate, the Holy Spirit, working in me. Give me boldness to confront when confrontation is needed. Make me a voice for the voiceless. Help me to confront with love, wisdom, clarity, dignity, and pure motives. Let my voice be heard by my leaders. Don't let any roots of bitterness spring up in my heart. Heal any hurts in my heart that might hinder my words from being heard. Give me the courage to confront my own weaknesses and correct my own mistakes. Give me the courage to speak up to obtain my promises, to claim my rightful spiritual and natural inheritance. Give me eyes to see the big picture. Lord, give me the counsel of Your Holy Spirit so that I might know when I need to confront and when I need to let something go. When I fight for what is right, I pray that You will look favorably on me so that my purpose will be accomplished.

DECLARATIONS TO AWAKEN A HEART FOR JUSTICE

I am an advocate for justice and righteousness.

I am a voice for the voiceless.

My leaders will hear my voice.

I will receive my rightful inheritance.

I will not be afraid to speak up.

I will not be passive.

I will confront with love, wisdom, clarity, courage, and tenacity.

I cooperate with authority to overcome injustice.

I am influential.

I seek the counsel of the Lord.

I fight the right cause with the right spirit and the right perspective.

Let justice run down like water and righteousness like a mighty stream.

Chapter 6

GOD'S BEST AND NOTHING LESS

Legendary Women Are Master Negotiators

A woman of grace and fire does not
manipulate but she is able to negotiate.

—FUNKE FELIX-ADEJUMO

THE LEGENDARY WOMAN has a God-given gift of being a master in the art of negotiation. She knows the value of perseverance, and she will not give up when God has asked her to pursue a certain course of action or opportunity. Her negotiation skills and the perseverance that backs them are critical in her pursuit of her God-given purpose. The legendary woman refuses to settle for anything less than God's best for her.

Merriam-Webster defines *negotiate* as "to deal with (some matter or affair that requires ability for its successful handling)...to arrange for or bring about through conference, discussion, and compromise."[1] The legendary woman uses her ability as a negotiator to successfully handle or deal with the matter at hand. Through efficient discussion and appropriate compromise she is able to achieve her desired end. She uses finesse and savvy to get others on board to support her in pursuit of her calling from God. However, she also recognizes the difference between negotiation and manipulation. *Manipulate* is defined as "to control or play upon by artful, unfair, or insidious means especially to one's own advantage."[2] The legendary woman is not a manipulator. She negotiates with honesty, with clarity, and for honorable purposes.

Negotiation is not a skill that is often associated with or expected of women. And while statistics show that over the last few years, women have been negotiating as much as men in the workplace, women who negotiate, whether successfully or not, often have to contend with the negative result of being viewed as bossy or aggressive.[3] But legendary women are not the type to let that kind of negativity stop them. They have been called with a purpose, and they push forward with perseverance until that purpose is achieved.

The legendary woman possesses the confidence needed to negotiate because she knows where her value lies and she knows the source of her confidence. Because she knows the Lord and what He has done in her, she knows her worth. Because of the work of Jesus in her life, she is righteous in the sight of God, and "the righteous are bold as a lion" (Prov. 28:1). She knows that "the LORD will be [her] confidence" (Prov. 3:26). She also knows that "this is the confidence that we have in Him, that if we ask anything according to His will, He hears us. And if we know that He hears us, whatever we ask, we know that we have the petitions that we have asked of Him" (1 John 5:14–15). The legendary woman knows her value in the sight of God, and she knows what God has equipped her to do, and that gives her the confidence and courage to go before authority figures, whether warriors or kings, bosses or judges, to ask for what she wants.

A WOMAN OF GOOD UNDERSTANDING

One of the legendary women in the Bible who were master negotiators was Abigail. The Bible describes her as "a woman of good understanding" (1 Sam. 25:3). The word translated "understanding" means prudence, insight, understanding, or wisdom.[4] This is an important quality for the master negotiator. She must be a critical thinker. She must have insight into and understanding of the matter at hand, as well as wisdom and prudence to discern the best way to proceed. There was a stark contrast between Abigail and her husband, Nabal, a man who lived up to his name, which means fool.[5]

David, who was on the run from Saul, heard that Nabal was shearing his sheep. David and his men had treated Nabal's men very well, offering protection while they were in the fields with them, so David sent messengers to Nabal, asking for him to return the favor by giving some provisions to him and his men. It was a modest, well-timed, humble request. But instead of responding with kindness and generosity, even though he was wealthy and would have had plenty to share since it was a feast time, Nabal responded by spurning David's request and insulting him.

But Nabal didn't insult just anyone. He insulted a seasoned warrior who had done him a great service. So David, in what admittedly wasn't one of his finest moments, ordered his men to gear up for battle. Then David and four hundred of his men headed in the direction of Nabal's house to exact revenge. One of Nabal's workers filled Abigail in about what was happening, correctly assessing that Nabal was "a scoundrel" (1 Sam. 25:17). Even though Abigail knew her husband's character was not the greatest, she didn't want David to exact revenge on Nabal by killing him and all his men. She sprang into action and prepared for the arrival of David's men:

> Then Abigail made haste and took two hundred loaves of bread, two skins of wine, five sheep already dressed, five seahs of roasted grain, one hundred clusters of raisins, and two hundred cakes of figs, and loaded them on donkeys. And she said to her servants, "Go on before me; see, I am coming after you." But she did not tell her husband Nabal.
>
> —1 Samuel 25:18–19

Abigail's preparations made it clear that Nabal could have easily afforded to be generous to David and his men. She knew that her negotiations would be more successful if she righted the wrong committed by her husband by giving provisions to David and his men. And this can be a key to successful negotiations for the legendary woman. Taking steps to right any wrongs that could be a barrier to getting what you want is always a wise step.

Abigail knew her purpose, and she prepared accordingly. When David and his men drew near, Abigail went out to meet them. She acknowledged the facts, including the foolishness of her husband. She was humble and respectful, in contrast to her husband's treatment of David. The legendary woman knows the importance of presenting facts clearly and with respect and humility. If you let your emotions run away with you, it can derail your negotiation.

Abigail successfully negotiated for her husband and his men to be spared. She spoke with such gentleness and wisdom that David recognized that his rash decision to kill Nabal and his men was not the right thing to do. He told her, "Blessed is the LORD God of Israel, who sent you this day to meet me! And blessed is your advice and blessed are you, because you have kept me this day from coming to bloodshed and from avenging myself with my own hand" (1 Sam. 25:32–33).

Abigail was well prepared for the negotiation, but notice that she also had a bigger picture in view. She closed her statement to David by saying, "But when the LORD has dealt well with my lord, then remember your maidservant" (1 Sam. 25:31). Abigail, in wisdom and discernment, recognized that there was more to David than just a warrior on the run. And David in turn recognized that there was more to Abigail than just the wife of a fool. And when Nabal died just a few days later, Abigail became David's wife. Her wisdom, humility, and savvy negotiating skills ended up elevating her to a position of authority, for David eventually became king. When you negotiate with gentleness and wisdom, it can pave the way for even greater opportunities down the road.

THE POWER OF PERSISTENCE

Another biblical woman with masterful negotiating skills is the persistent widow. She was a character in a parable, and while Jesus may not have necessarily had a specific woman in mind when He told the parable, we do know that widows are important to the Lord. He sees them, and He wants justice for them, so it is possible that Jesus had a specific woman in mind, perhaps even His own mother, who was widowed sometime between when Jesus was twelve years old and when He started His earthly ministry. The parable reads:

> There was in a certain city a judge who did not fear God nor regard man. Now there was a widow in that city; and she came to him, saying, "Get justice for me from my adversary." And he would not for a while; but afterward he said within himself, "Though I do not fear God nor regard man, yet because this widow troubles me I will avenge her, lest by her continual coming she weary me."
> —LUKE 18:2–5

Jesus told this parable in a time when women didn't rank very high on the social scale, and widows ranked even lower than women in general. He painted a picture of a woman who, despite her social status, knew she had a just cause. She wanted justice, and she had the confidence and courage to ask for it. She persistently went with boldness before a corrupt authority figure, demonstrating her faith in the justice of her cause and in the God whose throne is founded on justice and righteousness (Ps. 89:14).

This is a key concept for the legendary woman. The character of the authority figure you need to negotiate with or present your cause to is of little consequence when God is on your side. If God is for you, who can be against you? The legendary woman may have to speak to an unscrupulous judge or an unethical boss, but she can still speak with confidence and boldness because she is backed by the righteousness and justice of God. She is bold as a lion.

The widow in the parable was also persistent. She didn't let the first no from the judge cause her to give up in defeat. She didn't let the second time the judge ignored her request for justice destroy her hope. She kept presenting her cause, prompting even an unjust judge to grant her justice. Her perseverance paid off.

The legendary woman possesses perseverance. When her cause is just and right, she will not give up in defeat just because an unjust authority figure told her no. She trusts in God, not man, and she keeps going until she fulfills the calling on her life. She raises her faith like a shield and proclaims the promises of God and the truth of His Word. And when her defining moment of masterful negotiation comes, she will be ready, and she will give all the glory to God for the great things He has done.

The legendary woman also does not let social barriers get in the way of her negotiation. A Gentile woman once approached Jesus for help for her demon-possessed daughter. Jesus responded that He had been sent to the sheep of Israel, but the woman didn't let that stop her. Her mother's heart would not take no for an answer. Her love for her daughter prompted her to continue negotiating with Jesus to get what she wanted. She acknowledged the facts—that she was indeed a Gentile—but she told Jesus, "Even the little dogs eat the crumbs which fall from their masters' table" (Matt. 15:27).

Her love for her daughter, her faith, her persistence, and her negotiating skills paid off:

Jesus answered and said to her, "O woman, great is your faith! Let it be to you as you desire." And her daughter was healed from that very hour.

—MATTHEW 15:28

When you are negotiating, obstacles of all kinds may be put in your way. But the legendary woman does not let that stop her. She uses her wisdom and insight to get over, around, or through any barrier to achieving her purpose. The most successful people will not take no for an answer if a yes is needed to succeed.

YOUR DEFINING MOMENT

Nigerian billionaire businesswoman Folorunso Alakija is a legendary woman of today. She started her career in the banking industry but then left to start her own highly successful fashion label. But then God opened a door for her to meet with the Nigerian petroleum minister. At first she was just trying to get a small contract from the government for catering or transport, but the government wasn't interested. They wanted Nigerian nationals who were interested in applying for oil licenses. Mrs. Alakija's initial reaction to this was disappointment, but then she realized that God had allowed her to get her foot in the door for a reason. So she applied for an oil license.[6]

But then a new petroleum minister took over, and Mrs. Alakija had to start the process all over again. After three years, three petroleum ministers, and three applications, she managed to convince the Nigerian government to grant her an oil license. However, the license they gave her was for an area offshore, where any potential oil reserves were deep underwater; apparently it was the area nobody else wanted. She then had to begin the process of finding technical partners to explore the area. It took three more years of asking, seeking, knocking, and negotiating before she finally found a company willing to come on board with her, and then it took three months to negotiate the contract. But Mrs. Alakija never gave up. She knew God had helped her get her foot in the door for a reason, and she wouldn't give up until she knew what that reason was. And then her company struck oil in that area that no one else wanted. And it wasn't just a little oil; it was oil in commercial quantity.[7]

I believe Mrs. Alakija's defining moment as a master negotiator came when she realized there was a reason God allowed her to get her foot in the door with the petroleum minister. She made the decision in that moment to keep pressing forward for whatever God had for. She would be persistent. She would persevere. She would be bold, confident, and courageous, knowing that God was with her and for her. And the success she achieved because of that moment of decision was remarkable. And that is what legendary women do. When they recognize that God has opened a door or provided a new opportunity, they don't give up until they discover the reason God opened that door.

In an interview Mrs. Alakija said, "I thank God that I'm not the kind of person that you can push over....I will stand my ground. I will make my point known; I will drive it home. And I'm ready to face challenges....Through the grace of God, with Him being my Helper, there is no challenge that cannot be surmounted."[8]

Legendary woman, with God as your Helper there is no challenge that you cannot overcome. God has given you masterful negotiating skills backed by the boldness that comes from knowing you are right with Him. You can go before kings and all in authority with confidence and ask for what you want or need for yourself or to advance the kingdom of God. Remember, "the LORD will be your confidence" (Prov. 3:26).

Your defining moment as a master negotiator may come when you are asking for a raise or a promotion, when you are closing a big business deal, when you are asking for justice for yourself or someone you love, or when you are stepping out in faith to launch your ministry to a new level. It could be a moment with huge ramifications in the natural, in the spirit, or both. Your defining moment could be an actual negotiation, or it could be the moment when you realize that because of your value in Christ, you have the confidence to ask for what you want.

> Ask, and it will be given to you; seek, and you will find; knock, and it will be opened to you. For everyone who asks receives, and he who seeks finds, and to him who knocks it will be opened.
>
> —MATTHEW 7:7–8

One of the best ways to prepare for your defining moment of masterful negotiation is to pursue righteousness, for it is the righteous who are bold as lions. Cultivate your relationship with the Lord, because He is your confidence. Practice perseverance by being persistent in your prayers to arm yourself with the understanding of the building blocks of negotiation. Negotiation skills can be developed. The legendary woman must develop skills to play the win-win game of negotiation. Here is a list of skills and qualities the legendary woman must develop to prepare for effective negotiation:

- preparation and planning
- knowledge of the subject matter being negotiated; know what you want
- ability to think clearly and rapidly under pressure
- ability to express thoughts clearly
- ability to listen well

- sound judgment and general intelligence
- integrity
- ability to persuade others
- open mind
- well-thought-out ideas
- ability to articulate well (take a speech class if needed)
- perseverance
- patience
- assertiveness
- ability to stay detached emotionally
- flexibility
- insight (make sure you understand the other side)

Be ready for when your moment comes. Don't put limits on yourself. Be confident in who you are by knowing whose you are. Use your wisdom and your critical thinking skills to negotiate. Don't let the character or lack thereof of the one you are negotiating with make you afraid. Step out in faith and ask for what you want. And be persistent. Don't give up. Don't settle for less than God's best for you. You are a legendary woman, and you are worth it.

When Folorunso Alakija was asked about the legacy she wants to leave for her children and grandchildren, she didn't talk about money or property or businesses. She said she wanted to leave them a legacy of tenacity. She said, "The fact that you failed in something doesn't mean you failed forever."[9]

You will leave a legacy as well. You can pass on a heritage of confidence, boldness, and courage to your natural and spiritual heirs. Through your masterful negotiating skills you can demonstrate the power of knowing your value, your worth, because of what God has done in and through you. You can be a living example of the righteous woman who is bold as a lion. You can leave a powerful legacy of persistence, perseverance, and tenacity for other legendary women to follow.

PRAYER FOR THE GRACE AND WISDOM OF A MASTER NEGOTIATOR

Father God, just as it was with Jesus, let grace pour from my lips. Make my tongue like the pen of a ready writer. God, give me the tongue of the learned that I may speak a word in season to those who are weary. Empower me to articulate Your heart and mind with boldness and confidence. Fill my heart with forcible right words for occasions of my life. When I am faced with challenges, let me not cower in fear. Give me tenacity to finish every assignment and opportunity. Let my heart overflow with words of wisdom and authority. Give me the ability to persuade others to help in the advancement of the kingdom.

DECLARATIONS TO AFFIRM THE MASTER NEGOTIATOR IN YOU

I am a master negotiator.

I will ask for what God says I can have.

I decree that every muzzle is removed from my mouth.

I won't be muzzled by inferiority complexes.

I will pursue, overtake, and recover all.

I have favor with God and favor with mankind.

I will have an open mind.

I am a critical thinker.

I will think like God.

I will speak with authority but carry a demeanor of humility.

I loose myself from low self-worth.

I break every self-imposed limitation.

I will see my life from God's perspective.

I will have confidence in God and His abilities in me.

I have spiritual insight into the future.

I use my gift of discernment to capitalize on every God-led negotiation.

I am a visionary!

I will use the right, faith-focused words.

I have tenacity. I will stand until I have what the Lord has promised me!

Chapter 7

A HEART OF WISDOM

Legendary Women Are Discerning and Wise

You acquire wisdom at the cost of long years. You gain
wisdom at the price of obedience and perseverance.
You buy wisdom with the currency of suffering in
Christ.

—JONI EARECKSON TADA

DISCERNMENT AND WISDOM are key traits of the legendary woman. Women are often known for their wisdom, and we are all familiar with concepts such as women's intuition. A *Psychology Today* article (written by a man) asked whether women's intuition was a myth or reality. And the answer was "reality." The article pointed to the fact that women are generally better at reading facial expressions and are thus better at discerning the emotions of others. Women also tend to be better at expressing emotions and empathizing with others.[1]

Wisdom is different from intelligence. Wisdom is connected to good sense, insight, and sound judgment. People who are wise make an effort to learn from their life experiences and then apply that learning to their lives going forward. This is in contrast to fools, who do not learn from their mistakes.

> As a dog returns to his own vomit, so a fool repeats his
> folly.
>
> —PROVERBS 26:11

The Bible tells us that "fools despise wisdom and instruction" (Prov. 1:7). Foolishness, or folly, is connected to death, shame, grief, and destruction (Prov. 1:32; 3:35; 9:6; 10:1, 21; 13:20). The legendary woman is anything but a fool. She seeks wisdom and understanding, and she applies them to her life. She is grateful for opportunities to learn and grow, and she listens to wise counsel.

The wisdom and discernment women tend to have is the reason so many husbands have received one particular piece of advice: "Listen to your wife." This is not to say that wives are always right or that husbands shouldn't be leaders in the home. But women do possess wisdom that men would be wise to heed. As a matter of fact, in the Bible, wisdom is personified over and over again as a woman, even by Jesus Himself (e.g., Prov. 1:20; 8:1, 11; 9:1; Matt. 11:19; Luke 7:35).

THE WISE WOMAN

There is a clear connection between women and wisdom, but what does that mean? What does it mean to be a wise woman?

Proverbs says, "The wise woman builds her house, but the foolish pulls it down with her hands" (14:1). The word translated "builds" means to establish, to repair, to restore, to build up.[2] The wise woman is one whose words and actions edify and build up, repair and restore, establish and make strong. But it's not just about physical building, for the word translated "house," which usually refers to either a physical building or a household, can also mean "on the inside" or "within."[3] So the wise woman does not just build physically, but she also builds spiritually. While the wise legendary woman builds and manages her physical household well, she also is engaged in building up herself and others spiritually, with actions and words that bring edification, healing, and restoration. This is in direct contrast to the foolish woman, whose own words and actions bring destruction, overthrow, and ruin.[4]

The Bible speaks of the importance of wisdom over and over again:

> When wisdom enters your heart, and knowledge is pleasant to your soul, discretion will preserve you; understanding will keep you.
>
> —PROVERBS 2:10–11

> Wisdom is the principal thing; therefore get wisdom. And in all your getting, get understanding.
>
> —PROVERBS 4:7

> For wisdom is better than rubies, and all the things one may desire cannot be compared with her.
>
> —PROVERBS 8:11

> Wisdom brings success.
>
> —ECCLESIASTES 10:10

But when the Word of God talks about wisdom, it is talking about a very specific kind of wisdom with a very specific source. It is talking about the wisdom of God, not the wisdom of the world. In fact 1 Corinthians expressly states, "The wisdom of this world is foolishness with God" (3:19).

I realize you might be thinking you are lacking in the wisdom department, but the Bible makes it pretty clear how you can get wisdom. Colossians 3:16 says, "Let the word of Christ dwell in you richly in all wisdom." Digging into the Word of God and writing it on the tablet of your heart is a great way to get wisdom. But there is actually an even easier way: just ask for it.

> If any of you lacks wisdom, let him ask of God, who gives to all liberally and without reproach, and it will be given to him.
>
> —JAMES 1:5

That is an amazing promise. If you feel as if you lack wisdom, just ask God. Not only will He give it to you, but He will give it to you in abundance! And an abundance of wisdom is one of the marks of the legendary woman. It is a gift given to her by God.

DISCERNMENT

The legendary woman also possesses discernment. *Merriam-Webster* defines *discernment* as "the quality of being able to grasp and comprehend what is obscure; skill in discerning."[5] *Discern* comes from words that mean to perceive rationally, to distinguish, to sift, or to determine.[6] Discernment is the ability to see things clearly, to distinguish things that others might overlook, and to sift through matters to determine what is really important.

The discernment of the legendary woman manifests in several different ways. Paul prayed for the Philippians that their love would "abound still more and more in knowledge and all discernment" (1:9). The Greek word used for *discernment* is *aisthēsis*. It refers to "perception, not only by the senses but by the intellect...moral discernment in ethical matters."[7] The legendary woman possesses moral discernment—the ability to discern between good and evil, righteous and unrighteous—an important quality in a world where there seems to be more and more shades of gray in moral and ethical matters. She doesn't allow political correctness to sway her definitions of right and wrong.

The Bible also talks about discerning time. In fact the Book of Ecclesiastes says that "a wise man's heart discerns both time and judgment" (8:5), and the same could be said of a wise woman's heart. The legendary woman discerns times and seasons, and thus is able to seize opportunities—whether for advancement, deliverance, protection, or breakthrough—for herself and her family that might otherwise be missed. The legendary woman's ability to discern the times and seasons allows her to strategically align with God's timing.

RAHAB AND ABIGAIL

Two wise and discerning legendary women in Scripture are Rahab and Abigail. We have already looked at these women in connection with their fiery faith and masterful negotiation skills. But both women also showed great wisdom and discernment, especially with regard to discerning the times and seasons.

Imagine living in the walled city of Jericho at the time of Rahab. The high, thick walls of the city have always given you a great sense of safety since the gates can be closed up tight, protecting the city from any enemies. But then you start to hear stories from the mighty men you've serviced in your field of work. They tell of a group of people who escaped from Egypt under miraculous circumstances. The waters of the Red Sea were pushed back, allowing the people to cross over safely, and then the waters closed back, drowning the Egyptian army who was in pursuit. Then you hear about how Sihon, king of the Amorites, refused to let this group of people pass through his land. He chose to attack them instead, thinking victory was guaranteed, but he was defeated and killed. Then another nearby king, Og of Bashan, was also defeated. This group of escapees had taken possession of the land of two kings.

As a citizen of Jericho who hears these stories, you have a choice to make. You can dismiss the stories as fairy tales, as wild exaggerations. You can reason that there must have been some kind of strange circumstances that allowed the people of Israel to achieve such victories—after all, the lands of Sihon and Og don't have walls like Jericho's. You can choose to dismiss the stories, thinking that if the children of Israel happen to come to Jericho, the walls will protect you. And there is no doubt that is what many residents of Jericho did. They used human reasoning to dismiss any nervousness or fear the stories stirred up; they dismissed any thoughts that the stories might be true.

But that was not the choice Rahab made. In her wisdom and discernment she recognized the truth behind the stories. Then the two Israelite spies showed up at her door. And when she was presented with an opportunity to either hide the Israelite spies or turn them in, not only did she exercise great faith but she also discerned the time and season. She recognized that something big was happening and change was coming. And because of that, she was strategic and intentional in her words and actions. She wisely decided to not turn over the spies to the king of Jericho, and she seized an opportunity for the deliverance and protection of her family. Her wisdom, her discernment, her faith, and her negotiating skills all played a role in sparing Rahab, her parents, and her brothers and sisters when the Israelites defeated Jericho.

We are living in a time when change is coming, and just as Rahab did, you have a choice to make. You can use human reasoning as the basis of your decisions, or you can use your God-given wisdom and discernment to act strategically and in alignment with God's plans and purposes for you, your family, and His kingdom. Legendary woman, it is time to rise up in faith, act in wisdom, and seize the opportunities God is giving you.

Rahab's name comes from a word that can mean at liberty or proud.[8] Her defining moment of wisdom and discernment, when she chose to hide the spies, radically changed the trajectory of her life. She went from worshipping false gods to worshipping the one true God. And she stepped into the meaning of her name. No longer in the prison of prostitution and the shame that came with it, she stepped into freedom, into liberty as a proud wife and mother, one who would be an ancestor of Jesus Christ. And when you choose to follow the Lord, when you choose to rely on His wisdom for your strategy to fulfill your purpose, you will also walk in freedom.

Abigail also showed great wisdom and discernment. When she learned of her husband's behavior, she was wise enough to know that the consequences could be extreme. She immediately went into action, coming up with a wise plan to save her husband and his men. Just as Rahab did, Abigail seized an opportunity for the protection and deliverance of her family. And as we have already noted, Abigail's discernment allowed her to recognize that there was more to David than just a warrior on the run. And the long-term result of that wisdom and discernment was that Abigail became the wife of a king.

Legendary woman, the Holy Spirit will give you the gift of discerning of spirits. One of the major enemies to women is the spirit of deception. Just as the Lord gave the sons of Issachar the anointing to understand the times and seasons and to know exactly what to do, He is releasing this gift to you. The Holy Spirit will empower you to be creative, strategic, and intentional.

Legendary women recognize that acting with wisdom and discernment produces both short- and long-term results. They understand the law of sowing and reaping, so they know that when they sow seeds of wisdom, they will not reap the fruit of foolishness. Woman of God, in a world in which foolishness abounds, it is all the more important that you are consistently sowing seeds of wisdom. You may not always see the fruit right away, but in the end you will reap what you have sown (Gal. 6:7).

LEARNING LIFE LESSONS

Wise legendary women are also those who have keen insight into what the Lord is showing them through their experiences. They are quick to see life lessons, and they share them with others, which is why they make great mentors. These are the legendary women who often have suffered much, but they still keep a strong grip on the joy of the Lord. They treasure their experiences and ponder them in their hearts so they might know and understand the ways of the Lord. And truth be told, there are many wise legendary women like this. God has given them eyes to see and ears to hear, and they are sensitive to the Spirit of God at work in their lives.

One such woman was Corrie ten Boom. She was a legendary woman of fiery faith, fierce love, and amazing wisdom. Corrie and her family helped many Jews escape from the Nazis by hiding them in their home. They knew the danger they were putting themselves in, but they also knew they had to do what God was calling them to do. The family was betrayed, and they were arrested by the Gestapo. Corrie and her sister were sent to Ravensbrück concentration camp, where her sister died. But Corrie was released shortly after her sister's death—just one week before all the women her age were killed—due to a clerical error.

But what was an error on the part of a man was part of God's plan, for the Lord knew that Corrie was a legendary woman who would share the wisdom she gleaned from her experiences with literally millions. She wrote, "I know that the experiences of our lives, when we let God use them, become the mysterious and perfect preparation for the work He will give us to do."[9] And Corrie's experiences were her preparation for the work God gave her to do. Her wisdom impacted countless other legendary women and is an important part of her legacy of faith. Here are just a few nuggets of Corrie's wisdom:

Joy runs deeper than despair.[10]

There is no pit so deep that God's love is not deeper still.[11]

> Forgiveness is an act of the will, and the will can function regardless of the temperature of the heart.[12]

> Although the threads of my life have often seemed knotted, I know, by faith, that on the other side of the embroidery there is a crown.[13]

One of the most important things you can do to develop wisdom is to learn from your experiences. When God is trying to teach you something, it is better to learn it the first time so you can move on to other lessons rather than having to repeat the same lesson over and over again. Gaining a heart of wisdom takes effort, but it is worth the effort.

YOUR DEFINING MOMENT

Your defining moment of wisdom and discernment may be one that enables you to protect and deliver those you love because you correctly discern the time and season, much like Rahab and Abigail. It may be a moment when you realize that your season for going to a new level in your walk with the Lord has come. It may be a moment when you recognize, as Corrie ten Boom did, that the experiences of your life were preparing you to do His will, to fulfill His calling for your life. It may be a moment when you realize the wisdom God has given you has profoundly impacted others and grown the kingdom of God.

Regardless of what your moment looks like, it will allow you to pass on a legacy of wisdom to other legendary women. In his letter to Titus, the apostle Paul admonished the older women to teach the young women good things (2:3–5). Legendary woman, God has given you wisdom, taught you key lessons, and given you insight, all of which are of great value to others. And God has told you to pass on your wisdom. It doesn't matter whether you are young or old, physically or spiritually. Even if you are a young woman or a woman who is young in her faith, you still have wisdom, and that wisdom is powerful. The wisdom God has granted you is a gift. It is more valuable than rubies. You can use it to speak words of life that edify, build up, repair, heal, restore, and make strong.

To prepare for your defining moment of wisdom and discernment, you need to "gain a heart of wisdom" (Ps. 90:12). Spending time reading and meditating on Proverbs 8 is a critical component of gaining wisdom. Also pray and ask the Lord for wisdom. Ask Him to open your eyes, ears, and heart to the things He is teaching you. Ask Him to allow you to see the big picture when you are facing challenges. Ask Him to give you discernment of the times and seasons. Ask Him to make you abound in knowledge and discernment.

Ask Him to write His Word in your mind and on your heart. God is faithful. He will keep His promise and give you in abundance the wisdom you ask for. And when God gives you these gifts, treasure them. Ponder them in your heart. Use them to increase your faith and the faith of others. Use the truth of what God shows and teaches you to encourage and strengthen yourself in the Lord when troubles come (1 Sam. 30:6).

Legendary woman, you have wisdom from God. Use it to fulfill your purpose.

PRAYER FOR A DISCERNING HEART

Lord Jesus, make me a wise and discerning woman. Let me speak of excellent things, right things, and truth. Let my words be righteous, with nothing crooked or perverse in them. Lord, Your wisdom is better than rubies. Lord, give me prudence, knowledge, and discretion. Let me hate evil, pride, and arrogance. God, give me Your wise counsel and sound wisdom. Give me understanding and strength. Lord, I will diligently seek wisdom, and I will find it. I love Your wisdom;

it is better than gold. Because of the wisdom You have given me, I will have riches, honor, righteousness, and justice. Lord, I will hear Your instruction and be wise; I will not disdain it. I will not wrong my own soul by hating wisdom. I will be blessed because I listen to You, and I will find life and obtain Your favor.

DECLARATIONS TO AWAKEN WISDOM AND DISCERNMENT

I am wise and discerning.

I am not foolish. I learn from my mistakes.

I seek wisdom and understanding.

My words and actions build up rather than tear down.

The Word dwells in me richly in all wisdom.

When I ask for wisdom, God gives it to me in abundance.

I have moral discernment.

I have the gift of discerning of spirits.

I will not be deceived.

I act strategically and in alignment with God's plans and purposes.

I discern the times and seasons.

I will learn what God is teaching me.

I will gain a heart of wisdom.

Chapter 8

GOING ABOVE AND BEYOND

Legendary Women Are Extravagant Givers

One can give without loving, but one cannot love
without giving.

—AMY CARMICHAEL

PHILANTHROPY IS A key trait for legendary women.
Whether out of her abundance or even out of her lack, the
legendary woman is an extravagant giver. She ministers to
the Lord out of her substance. She gives willingly and cheerfully,
knowing that "God loves a cheerful giver" (2 Cor. 9:7).

The legendary woman's giving starts with the basics: she
tithes. She gives 10 percent of her income back to the Lord. For
the legendary woman, tithing is a spiritual discipline, much
like spending time in the Word, in worship, and in prayer. But
it is more than that. It is also an act of obedience, which also
means it is an act of love. And because it is an act of love, it is
also an act of worship.

Tithing is also an act of trust, especially for those who
might be struggling to make ends meet. When you tithe, you
are telling the Lord that you trust Him to do more with 90
percent than you could do with 100 percent. The legendary
woman is not hindered by fear when it comes to her giving.
She knows one of the names of God is the Lord your Provider,
and she has experienced the truth behind that name in her life.
She fully trusts the Lord to provide for her needs. It is also
worthy of note that tithing is the only thing that God ever said
to test Him on:

> "Bring all the tithes into the storehouse, that there may
> be food in My house, and try Me now in this," says the
> LORD of hosts, "if I will not open for you the windows
> of heaven and pour out for you such blessing that there
> will not be room enough to receive it."
>
> —MALACHI 3:10

But the legendary woman's giving goes beyond tithing. She is an extravagant giver, meaning that she also gives offerings to the Lord that are above and beyond her tithe. And please know that the amount doesn't have to have a lot of zeros on the end for it to be an extravagant gift. When Jesus was in the temple one day, He saw a "poor widow" putting two mites into the treasury (Luke 21:2). The word translated "poor" in that verse comes from a word that means indigent, someone who has to toil for daily subsistence.[1] A mite was the smallest and least valuable coin, so if you view it from that perspective, her gift was two cents. If you view it as a percentage of a day's wages, the two mites would probably be around a dollar today. Either way, the gift was quite insignificant in monetary terms. But for a widow living in an era when widows had no way of supporting themselves and were dependent on the kindness of others for survival, the gift was extravagant. Jesus said, "Truly I say to you that this poor widow has put in more than all; for all these out of their abundance have put in offerings for God, but she out of her poverty put in all the livelihood that she had" (Luke 21:3–4).

The poor widow was faithful with little. And that is where many legendary women start. They are faithful with their finances, whether they have little or much. But it is a spiritual truth that "one who is faithful in a very little is also faithful in much" (Luke 16:10, ESV). Legendary women honor God with their finances, so He knows He can trust them with abundance.

And with their extravagant giving, legendary women could be used to fund the next great move of God.

The legendary woman is not hindered by selfishness when it comes to her giving. As God has been generous to her, so she is generous to others. She knows the truth of Proverbs 11:25: "The generous soul will be made rich, and he who waters will also be watered himself." She sows bountifully and will also reap bountifully (2 Cor. 9:6). She does not let greed or covetousness build up in her heart. She takes seriously the warning about having your heart in the wrong place with regard to your finances:

> For the love of money is a root of all kinds of evil, for which some have strayed from the faith in their greediness, and pierced themselves through with many sorrows.
> —1 Timothy 6:10

The legendary woman is not hindered by selfishness or greed, because she keeps the Lord in first place in her heart. She serves Him, not money (Matt. 6:24). Because she keeps her heart in the right place, she is able to give extravagantly.

The Ministry of Giving

The Gospel of Luke names several women who supported Jesus with their giving:

> Now it came to pass, afterward, that He went through every city and village, preaching and bringing the glad tidings of the kingdom of God. And the twelve were with Him, and certain women who had been healed of evil spirits and infirmities—Mary called Magdalene, out of whom had come seven demons, and Joanna the wife of Chuza, Herod's steward, and Susanna, and many others who provided for Him from their substance.
> —Luke 8:1–3

So there was a group of women who were providing for the physical needs of Jesus as He traveled throughout the area, preaching the gospel. The support the women provided out of their substance, their wealth and possessions, allowed Jesus to focus on fulfilling His mission and doing what He was called to do. The word translated "provided" in Luke 8:3 is *diakoneō*. It means to serve, to supply food and necessities of life, or to wait upon.[2] It is the same word used for deacons, who are the designated doers of the church. Deacons and deaconesses serve and take care of the practical needs of the church so that apostles, pastors, teachers, and elders can focus on teaching the Word of God. And just as deacons and deaconesses are often serving behind the scenes, those who support a ministry through their giving are often behind the scenes as well. But that does not mean they are not a vital part of a ministry. Because while *diakoneō* means to serve or supply the needs of, it also means to minister.[3]

The support Mary, Joanna, Susanna, and the others gave to Jesus was ministry. It was their ministry. You don't need to have a spotlight on you or be up on a platform to have a ministry. When you are faithful to do the things God has called you to do, whatever form they take, you are involved in ministry. The apostle Paul explained it like this:

> For as we have many members in one body, but all the members do not have the same function, so we, being many, are one body in Christ, and individually members of one another. Having then gifts differing according to the grace that is given to us, let us use them: if prophecy, let us prophesy in proportion to our faith; or ministry, let us use it in our ministering; he who teaches, in teaching; he who exhorts, in exhortation; he who gives, with liberality; he who leads, with diligence; he who shows mercy, with cheerfulness.
>
> —Romans 12:4–8

Notice that Paul named giving in the same list of gifts with prophesying and teaching, gifts we tend to hold in high esteem. But being an extravagant giver is just as much of a gift as prophesying and teaching. Paul also wrote:

> There are diversities of gifts, but the same Spirit. There are differences of ministries, but the same Lord.
> —1 CORINTHIANS 12:4–5

So if you have the gift of giving, don't view it as a lesser gift. Those who give generously, graciously, and cheerfully are vital to the work of the kingdom. They have been entrusted by God to be good stewards of the blessings He has given them. And the rewards of their generosity are great:

> Remember this: Whoever sows sparingly will also reap sparingly, and *whoever sows generously will also reap generously.* Each of you should give what you have decided in your heart to give, not reluctantly or under compulsion, for *God loves a cheerful giver.* And *God is able to bless you abundantly*, so that in all things at all times, having all that you need, *you will abound in every good work.* As it is written: "They have freely scattered their gifts to the poor; *their righteousness endures forever.*"
>
> Now he who supplies seed to the sower and bread for food will also *supply and increase your store of seed and will enlarge the harvest of your righteousness.* You will be *enriched in every way* so that you can be generous on every occasion, and through us *your generosity will result in thanksgiving to God.*
>
> This service that you perform is not only supplying the needs of the Lord's people but is also overflowing in many expressions of thanks to God. Because of the service by which you have proved yourselves, *others will praise God* for the obedience that accompanies your confession of the gospel of Christ, and for your generosity in

sharing with them and with everyone else. And in their prayers for you *their hearts will go out to you*, because of the surpassing grace God has given you. Thanks be to God for his indescribable gift!
—2 CORINTHIANS 9:6–15, NIV, EMPHASIS ADDED

Those are some amazing rewards. The gift of giving is indeed indescribable.

As a legendary woman, you may not be the one preaching the gospel, you may not be the one on the platform, but you can still be legendary by supporting the one who is. The legendary woman is one who is willing to fulfill the call of God on her life, whether she is out front or behind the scenes.

Looking back at the verses from the Gospel of Luke, once again the meanings of the names of the women paint a picture of the extravagant giver. The Greek word for *Susanna* means lily.[4] It comes from a Hebrew word that also means lily, but its root word means cheerful.[5] Joanna means "Jehovah is a gracious giver."[6] The second part of Mary's name, Magdalene, means she was from Magdala. But the word itself means tower.[7] The Greek word traces back to the Hebrew word *migdāl*, which also means tower but can also mean pulpit or platform.[8] So we have a picture of women who gave cheerfully, for that is what God loves. And they gave in response to God's own gracious giving to them, an act of gratitude, love, and worship. And their giving was in support of Jesus, the One on the platform, the One who was behind the pulpit.

That is also the picture of the legendary woman who is an extravagant giver. She gives cheerfully. She gives in response to the goodness that God has shown her, for He is indeed a gracious giver. And even though she may not be on the platform herself, she is willing to support whoever is.

YOUR DEFINING MOMENT

Your defining moment of extravagant giving as a legendary woman could look many different ways. God could open up the storehouse of heaven and pour out such abundance on you in a moment of time that it redirects your course to become a philanthropist who gives generously wherever and however God directs. Your moment could be when an extraordinarily gifted minister of the gospel crosses your path in a divine encounter, and the Holy Spirit lets you know that minister is the one you are to support with your giving. Your defining moment could be when you are struggling to pay the bills, but the Holy Spirit prompts you to give extravagantly, be it two dollars or two hundred or two thousand, and you choose to trust and obey. Or your moment could be when you come face to face with something that breaks your heart or stirs up a desire to see wrongs righted or resonates so deeply in your soul that you know you have found your calling.

For Elizabeth Fry, that moment was when she visited Newgate Prison for the first time. It was 1813, and the conditions in the prison were deplorable. There were three hundred women in a space of about 190 square yards. They slept on the floor without any kind of bedding, and many of the women lacked basic clothing. It was a filthy, fearsome place, and the man in charge wouldn't even enter it unless he had a guard to protect him. But Elizabeth Fry knew she had found her purpose, her call from God. She entered and said to the prisoners, "You seem unhappy; you are in want of clothes: would you be pleased if some one were to come and relieve your misery?" The women of course said they would, but they didn't believe anyone cared for them. But Mrs. Fry offered them hope, and even though the women didn't believe she would ever return to the prison, she did.[9]

Elizabeth Fry became an advocate for prison reform, giving

of her time, her money, and herself to help prisoners. She helped push for legislation to improve treatment of prisoners, even giving evidence in Parliament (the first woman to do so) on prison conditions. But she also gave extravagantly. It is estimated that she gave over thirty thousand pounds during the course of her lifetime to help those who were imprisoned, in need of help, and in need of hope. Today that would amount to nearly five million dollars.

You may not have five million dollars. You may not even have five dollars in your bank account at the moment. But the extravagant giving of the legendary woman starts with her heart. Because she loves the Lord, she wants to give as an act of obedience, love, and worship. She recognizes that everything she has was given to her by God, and she wants to steward it well. And so the legendary woman starts by tithing. She remembers what Jesus said in the Sermon on the Mount:

> Look at the birds of the air, for they neither sow nor reap nor gather into barns; yet your heavenly Father feeds them. Are you not of more value than they?
> —MATTHEW 6:26

The legendary woman knows she is valuable in the sight of God, so she is not hindered by fear or worry. She takes that first step of trust and obedience, and she tithes. And as God blesses that obedience, she keeps her heart in the right place. She does not allow selfishness or greed to develop in her heart. With her eyes fixed on Jesus and her trust steadfastly planted in His faithfulness, she cheerfully begins to give more. God has poured out love on her, so she wants to pour out her love on Him by giving generously to further the work of His kingdom. The extravagant giving of the legendary woman begins when she is faithful with little; she will also be faithful with much.

Woman of God, you are living in a time when financial ups

and downs are having a significant impact on the work of the kingdom. For example, the COVID-19 pandemic resulted in many churches and ministries, especially small ones, having to close their doors. Your extravagant giving, especially combined with the extravagant giving of other legendary women, has the power to prevent that. Pray and ask the Lord which ministry or ministries He wants you to sow into. Then follow His leading and give extravagantly.

The legendary woman will leave a legacy of philanthropy and extravagant giving. Her natural and spiritual children will see her good works, and not only will they praise the Father in heaven but they will also be inspired by her generosity. Generosity is contagious. And beyond that, when the legendary woman gives extravagantly to the work of the kingdom, it has far-reaching effects that will last for eternity.

While this chapter has focused on extravagant giving of finances and substance, the truth is that the legendary woman also gives extravagantly of herself, not just of her financial resources but also of her time, her faith, her love, her wisdom, and her heart. She is willing to be poured out as a drink offering to her Lord, and that is the most extravagant gift of all.

PRAYER TO AWAKEN A GENEROUS HEART

Lord Jesus, I pray that You will give me a heart of generosity that I might be an extravagant giver. Whether out of my abundance or out of my lack, I will give cheerfully to bless Your heart. I will tithe as an act of obedience, an act of love, and an act of worship. I trust You to provide for my needs, and I will not be hindered by fear when it comes to giving. You are the Lord my Provider. I will not be selfish or greedy. As You have been generous to me, so I will be generous to others. Let me sow and reap bountifully.

Lord, I want to support the work of Your kingdom with my giving. I don't have to be on the platform to be involved in ministry; I just have to be faithful to do what You have called me to do. Help me to be a good steward of the blessings You have given me. God, I trust You to keep Your promise that when I sow abundantly and cheerfully, You will bless me abundantly, increase my store of seed, and enlarge the harvest of my righteousness.

DECLARATIONS TO AFFIRM THE EXTRAVAGANT GIVER WITHIN

I am an extravagant giver.

I tithe, giving God the first 10 percent of my income.

I give of my substance.

I give of myself.

I give as an act of obedience, love, and worship.

I give because I am thankful.

I am a good steward of my blessings.

I am generous.

I am a cheerful giver.

I sow generously and will reap generously.

I give to support the work of the kingdom.

Giving is a ministry.

I am faithful with little and faithful with much.

The Lord will increase my store of seed and enlarge the harvest of my righteousness.

I will leave a legacy of extravagant giving.

Chapter 9

PASSIONATE FOR HIS PRESENCE

Legendary Women Live Poured-Out Lives

We receive His poured-out life and, being allowed the
high privilege of suffering with Him, may then pour
ourselves out for others.

—Elisabeth Elliot

T HE LEGENDARY WOMAN lives a poured-out, surrendered, yielded life before her Maker. Greatly forgiven, delivered from death and destruction, rescued from enemies and foes, wholly accepted, and lovingly redeemed, she has great love for the Master. She will go where He says to go and do what He says to do. She spends time in His presence, at His feet, pouring out her love for Him, knowing that she can love Him only because He loved her first.

The legendary woman remembers where she has been. She remembers the things that held her in bondage and weighed her down with guilt and shame. But she also remembers the moment her Lord and Savior unlocked her shackles, loosed her chains, opened the prison door, and lovingly called out, "Awake, awake, O captive daughter! Shake yourself from the dust. Arise. You are free. Stand fast in the freedom by which I have made you free." (See Isaiah 52:1–2 and Galatians 5:1.)

Because of all that the Lord has done for her, the legendary woman can't help but worship. She has been redeemed by His love. She has been overwhelmed by His grace. She has been captivated by His goodness. She has been showered with His blessings. She has been humbled by His mercy. Her response is to worship Him and praise Him, saying, "For He is good, for His mercy endures forever" (2 Chron. 7:3). She enters His gates with thanksgiving and His courts with praise; she is thankful to Him and blesses His name (Ps. 100:4).

The legendary woman's worship is not hindered by ingratitude. She is so thankful for what the Lord has done for her, both the big things and the little things. She has stored up His wondrous deeds on her behalf in her heart like treasures. She will not forget them, and she will not forget to bless the name of the Lord for all the good He has done.

The legendary woman does not abandon the love she had for Jesus at first (Rev. 2:4). She is not lukewarm (Rev. 3:16). She is not in a state of spiritual boredom or complacency. She will not be hindered by these things, because if she recognizes any of them developing in her heart, she immediately heads for the feet of Jesus. She stirs up her love by being with Him. Her passion for Jesus grows day by day as she spends time in His presence. Her faith and her love are both fiery and fierce. She is confident in her identity as the bride of Christ. She is His, and He is hers (Song of Sol. 2:16).

The legendary woman also presents her body as a living sacrifice, holy and acceptable to God, knowing that is her reasonable act of worship and service (Rom. 12:1). She is a willing vessel. She is clay in the hands of the master potter. She is His workmanship, and she wants to walk in the good works that God prepared beforehand just for her (Eph. 2:10).

The legendary woman gives extravagantly of herself. She is obedient, knowing that obedience is better than sacrifice. She has fierce love for her Savior. And in all these things she pours herself out like a drink offering, for a sweet aroma, an offering made to the Lord.

FOUND AT THE FEET OF JESUS

For biblical examples of legendary women who were poured out, we look to an unnamed woman and Mary of Bethany, both of whom were found at the feet of Jesus.

The Gospel of Luke recounts the following story:

> Then one of the Pharisees asked Him to eat with him. And He went to the Pharisee's house, and sat down to eat. And behold, a woman in the city who was a sinner, when she knew that Jesus sat at the table in the Pharisee's house, brought an alabaster flask of fragrant oil, and stood at His feet behind Him weeping; and she began to wash His feet with her tears, and wiped them with the hair of her head; and she kissed His feet and anointed them with the fragrant oil. Now when the Pharisee who had invited Him saw this, he spoke to himself, saying, "This Man, if He were a prophet, would know who and what manner of woman this is who is touching Him, for she is a sinner."
>
> And Jesus answered and said to him, "Simon, I have something to say to you."
>
> So he said, "Teacher, say it."
>
> "There was a certain creditor who had two debtors. One owed five hundred denarii, and the other fifty. And when they had nothing with which to repay, he freely forgave them both. Tell Me, therefore, which of them will love him more?"
>
> Simon answered and said, "I suppose the one whom he forgave more."
>
> And He said to him, "You have rightly judged." Then He turned to the woman and said to Simon, "Do you see this woman? I entered your house; you gave Me no water for My feet, but she has washed My feet with her tears and wiped them with the hair of her head. You gave Me no kiss, but this woman has not ceased to kiss My feet since the time I came in. You did not anoint My head

with oil, but this woman has anointed My feet with fragrant oil. Therefore I say to you, her sins, which are many, are forgiven, for she loved much. But to whom little is forgiven, the same loves little."

Then He said to her, "Your sins are forgiven."

And those who sat at the table with Him began to say to themselves, "Who is this who even forgives sins?"

Then He said to the woman, "Your faith has saved you. Go in peace."

—LUKE 7:36–50

The identity of the woman in this passage is unknown. Some say she was Mary Magdalene; others say she was Mary of Bethany. Some believe she was a prostitute or a woman who had been caught in adultery. But Luke chose to just identify her as a woman who was a sinner, because in reality her name or the nature of her sin isn't important. She is a woman all of us can relate to because we are all sinners; we "all have sinned and fall short of the glory of God" (Rom. 3:23). All of us are in need of mercy and grace and forgiveness so that we can be in right standing with the Lord God Almighty.

This legendary woman recognized her state. She recognized her sin. She recognized her need for forgiveness. And she recognized the One who freely offered that forgiveness. And there was nothing she could do except respond with an act of worship. So this legendary woman, who was widely known as a sinner, summoned up her God-given courage and walked into the house of a Pharisee. Her fierce love for the Lord prompted her to give extravagantly, purchasing a costly alabaster flask of fragrant oil with which to anoint the feet of Jesus. She walked into that house with faith that Jesus would accept her offering. And in her defining moment, she poured herself out as an act of love and worship.

It started with her tears. Her heart was so full that there was no place for the overflow to go except out of her eyes. She was

124

initially standing behind Jesus, but she couldn't stay there. She knelt at His feet, washing the dirt and filth from His feet with her tears. His grace had made her spiritually clean, had cleansed her from all unrighteousness; now she used the outpouring of her heart to make Jesus' feet physically clean. And the woman's tears were not just a drop or two silently and beautifully trickling down her face. When the Word says that "she began to wash His feet with her tears" (Luke 7:38), the word translated "wash" means to moisten by a shower or to rain.[1] The woman was ugly crying, sending a shower of tears onto the feet of Jesus.

Woman of God, never be ashamed of your tears. Tears of repentance, tears of overwhelming gratitude, tears of sorrow, tears of joy—they are all precious to God. He gathers them up in a bottle and records them in His book (Ps. 56:8).

The woman then used her hair to wipe His feet. The Bible talks about a woman's hair being her glory (1 Cor. 11:15). By using her hair to wipe Jesus' feet, the woman was acknowledging in an act of humility that her glory was nothing compared with the Lord. Any glory she had was worth sacrificing and pouring out in worship of the one true God. She understood that there was more glory in understanding and knowing the Lord, who exercises loving-kindness, judgment, and righteousness in the earth (Jer. 9:24). And she understood that true glory belongs to God and God alone. The legendary woman always gives the glory to God.

After she washed Jesus' feet with her tears and her hair, the woman kissed His feet. It was yet another act of worship. In fact the Greek word for *worship* means "to kiss the hand to (towards) one" or to prostrate oneself in reverence or adoration.[2] And the Greek word for *kiss* used in the passage in Luke means to kiss again and again.[3]

But the woman wasn't done. She then anointed Jesus' feet with fragrant oil. It was an offering, poured out on the feet of Jesus and producing a pleasing aroma. The oil was an expensive, extravagant gift. But it was worth it to show her devotion, her gratitude, and her love for Jesus. And it's worth noting that in the Greek the tense of the verbs *wipe*, *kiss*, and *anoint* in that one verse indicates an ongoing action. They weren't just acts of a moment; they continued. And that is at the heart of the legendary woman's worship. Her act of pouring herself out at the feet of Jesus—be it by extravagantly giving, loving fiercely, obeying without wavering, giving up her glory for the glory of the Lord, or any other act of worship—is ongoing. It never stops. It is an attitude of her heart. She is a living sacrifice. She is a drink offering, continually poured out as a pleasing aroma.

Another legendary woman found at the feet of Jesus was Mary of Bethany. She was the sister of Lazarus and Martha. Jesus had arrived in their village, and Martha had welcomed Him into her home. Mary "sat at Jesus' feet and heard His word" (Luke 10:39). Mary understood the importance of spending time in the presence of the Lord, and she wouldn't let anything cause her to miss out on an opportunity to do so. She was hungry for the Word. She had a heart to learn from Him. She had a heart of worship. And she was willing to pour herself out, to let go of what others expected her to be.

And Jesus commended her for that. When Martha complained that Mary wasn't helping her, He said, "But one thing is needed, and Mary has chosen that good part, which will not be taken away from her" (Luke 10:42). Mary chose well. She focused on being exactly who God called her to be, regardless of what others thought.

And that is what legendary women do. They die to themselves and to the opinions of others. They realize that the only expectations that really matter are God's. Both Mary and the unnamed woman understood that. They knew that the opinions of Pharisees and family members weren't what was important; what was important was to be at the feet of Jesus. So they defied cultural norms and expectations to spend time with the

Lord, to worship Him, to learn from Him, and to love Him. They poured themselves out.

Mary's story also has a cautionary tale for the legendary woman. Her sister, Martha, was a legendary woman of fiery faith in her own right. But Luke wrote that Martha "was distracted with much serving" (Luke 10:40). Legendary woman, God has given you many gifts, and He has called you to serve the body of Christ and His kingdom with those gifts. But you need to fulfill your purpose, your calling, not what other people think your calling or purpose is. You need to use your wisdom and discernment to go where God tells you to go and do what God tells you to do. It is all too easy for Satan to keep you from fulfilling your true purpose by having you do lots of other good things. Don't get caught up and distracted by much serving.

YOUR DEFINING MOMENT

It may at times be difficult for a legendary woman to pinpoint her defining moment of being poured out since it is an ongoing, continual process. Jesus is your magnificent obsession. You must follow Him wherever He goes. The day you realize that He is the only One who is holy, He is the only One who is good, when your heart is awakened with a burning desire to give everything to Him at any cost—that's your defining moment, the time when you pledge your allegiance to Jesus.

Legendary woman, you are called to live a life poured out, surrendered, and yielded before your Maker. In this day and age that could look many different ways. But one thing is certain: the poured-out legendary woman gives of herself extravagantly to worship and serve the Lord.

Legendary women who are pouring themselves out have key moments that are evidence of the ongoing process, moments that clearly demonstrate their love, faith, and obedience, moments that are a demonstration of the lives they are pouring out as drink offerings to their Lord and Savior. They are defining moments. And I believe one of those defining moments came for legendary woman Fanny Crosby when she was ninety-two years old.

Crosby went blind when she was only six weeks old due to an eye infection and a lack of adequate medical care. But her blindness never stopped her from pursuing and fulfilling her calling from God. Over the course of her lifetime it is estimated she wrote between 5,500 and 9,000 hymns. The actual number is unknown because she used numerous pseudonyms. And the lyrics of her hymns—"Blessed Assurance," for example—attest to the fact that she was a woman pouring herself out in worship and adoration of her Lord:

> Blessed assurance, Jesus is mine;
> Oh, what a foretaste of glory divine!
> Heir of salvation, purchase of God,
> Born of His Spirit, washed in His blood.
>
> This is my story, this is my song,
> Praising my Savior all the day long.
> This is my story, this is my song,
> Praising my Savior all the day long.
>
> Perfect submission, perfect delight,
> Visions of rapture now burst on my sight;
> Angels descending, bring from above
> Echoes of mercy, whispers of love.
>
> Perfect submission, all is at rest,
> I in my Savior am happy and blest;
> Watching and waiting, looking above,
> Filled with His goodness, lost in His love.[4]

Crosby's hymns are evidence of what was in her heart. But she didn't just write hymns. She was willing to do whatever the Lord called her to do, from writing hymns and poems to visiting inner-city missions to working with outcasts to preaching the gospel on whatever platform the Lord gave her. In her autobiography, written when she was eighty-three, she responded to the question she was often asked about how long she expected to live:

> [I] am willing to stay as long as the good Lord has any work for me to do....Whenever the Lord calls me, I am willing to go; but if He chooses to leave me here...I shall continue to gather sheaves till the sun goes down, and to sing and write hymns to His praise.[5]

This is the heart of the poured-out legendary woman. She is willing to do whatever the Lord calls her to do for as long as He calls her to do it. Crosby was willing to continue gathering the harvest for the Lord by sharing the gospel and to continue offering the thoughts and meditations of her heart as an act of praise and worship to her God as long as He left her on earth.

What I believe was a defining moment of Crosby's poured-out life occurred when she was ninety-two years old, about two years before the Lord called her home. She had the opportunity to visit Cambridge, Massachusetts, where Harvard is located. While there she spoke at a church to a crowd of over two thousand people:

> I spoke to them from my very heart of that wonderful story of Jesus Christ who came into this world with a love big enough to fill every nook and corner of it, if only mankind would allow Him. It was a great service, the presence of Christ being felt both in the music and the message.
>
> I shall never forget that service to my dying day; and I think I shall remember when I join the Church Triumphant before God and the Lamb. When it was over I slept like a child at the joy of being able in story and in song to tell of my Saviour's boundless love.[6]

What a moment. At age ninety-two she wasn't sitting in a rocking chair, waiting on the Lord to call her home. She was standing on a platform in front of thousands, preaching the gospel, and she was filled with joy at just the thought of being able to tell others of the love of Jesus Christ.

I feel as if I had my own defining moment of being poured out not too long ago. God had directed me to move to Florida from Chicago, the only home I had ever known. It was life altering. Completely uprooting myself and moving to another state was a big step of faith on my part, but I believed I was obeying the voice of the Lord. And then the pandemic happened, and nothing was progressing the way I had expected it to. So I sat alone in my house and went to the feet of Jesus, asking Him if I had really heard from Him and done the right thing. And He told me, "Better is one day in My courts than a thousand elsewhere." (See Psalm 84:10.)

That is a profound truth that every legendary woman knows. Better is one day following the Lord and pursuing His purpose for your life than a thousand days doing anything else. Even when it doesn't make sense. Even when the world tells you that you're being foolish. Even when things don't go as planned. Even when being a living sacrifice is painful.

> One thing I have desired of the LORD, that will I seek:
> That I may dwell in the house of the LORD all the days of
> my life, to behold the beauty of the LORD, and to inquire
> in His temple.
>
> —PSALM 27:4

The legendary woman lives a devoted and lavishly worshipful life. Her worship is a vital component of her walk with the Lord. It is an act of love, a love that will not grow cold. It is an outpouring of what she holds in her heart. And when she pours out her heart, it opens her heart to the glory and prophetic moving of God.

You may recognize your defining moment when it comes, or it may just slip by unnoticed as just one of many moments in a life poured out in an ongoing process. But regardless of whether you notice, the Lord will. He is pleased by your worship. He is pleased by your devotion. When you present your body as a living sacrifice, when you are a drink offering poured out, your life is a fragrant aroma to the Lord. Worship is a lifestyle. And your life of worship is also part of your legacy. It will inspire others to want to spend time at the feet of Jesus, just as you have. And spending time at the feet of Jesus will change them, just as it has changed you. And your legacy will continue through them.

Prayer to Live a Poured-Out Life

Jesus, I love You with all of my heart. Draw me, and I will run after You. Let Your loving-kindness lead me into all truth. I am Yours, and You are mine. I thank You that I am no longer an orphan but have been accepted in the Beloved. I cry out, Abba, Father. I ask that You remove anything that will hinder my love for You. Let the fire in Your eyes burn Your love in my heart. Take out the stony heart and put in a heart of flesh. Jesus, I will serve You from a place of love and not duty. Holy Spirit, pour the love of God in my heart. Holy Spirit, teach me how to love the Lord with all of my heart. Your leadership of love abides over me, ending the search for significance in my soul! Your purpose for me is my heart's desire. I will not per-form for love because I already have it. I am important not because of what I do but because You paid for my soul with Your precious blood.

DECLARATIONS TO STIR A
PASSIONATE PURSUIT OF GOD

I will set my heart to love the Lord.

I make a decision to seek the Lord with all of my heart.

I choose to make loving the Lord my ultimate quest.

I will pursue loving the Lord and knowing Him, and blessing and assignments will follow.

Lord, teach me how to develop my bridal identity.

I don't work for the Lord, but I work with Him to fulfill my assignment in the earth.

God, break me free from compromise.

I decree that I will live with a fiery heart of love. I break off spiritual boredom, laziness, and complacency.

I set myself not to live from a place of lukewarmness. I will not live a life of mediocrity.

I will not settle for less than the fullness of God.

I will love the Lord with all my heart.

I break off confusion and half-heartedness.

I will set my affections on things above. I will live a life that brings heaven on earth.

I will not withhold anything the Lord has asked of me.

I want to live a life worthy of the Lord's suffering.

I will give God my time, talent, and tithes to further His plans and purposes in the earth.

Chapter 10

GOD'S SECRET WEAPON

Legendary Women Are Stealthy Warriors

No matter what your battle is, it is not yours; the battle
belongs to the Lord, and He has a plan to bring you
victory.

—JOYCE MEYER

THERE ARE TIMES when the legendary woman is called to be a woman of few words but great action. There are times when her calling means she needs to be stealthy, strong in her silence, and accurate in her action. The legendary woman is God's secret weapon. Sometimes hidden or meek or quiet or unassuming or behind-the-scenes, she is able to carry out successful assaults on the enemy, one after the other. She knows that she doesn't need the spotlight. She knows she doesn't need to broadcast her actions to the world. She knows she just needs to obey, and there is power in obedience.

The legendary woman is not just a hearer of the Word. She is a doer of the Word (Jas. 1:22–25). Familiar phrases such as "Actions speak louder than words" and "I can show you better than I can tell you" are accurate characterizations of the legendary woman. She is willing to use whatever she has at hand to defeat the enemy.

The legendary woman knows the truth of the scripture that says, "In quietness and confidence shall be your strength" (Isa. 30:15). She knows that the strongest person is not always the loudest. She has "the incorruptible beauty of a gentle and quiet spirit, which is very precious in the sight of God" (1 Pet. 3:4). She knows that words aren't always necessary because her heart is filled with the peace that passes all understanding and her actions are prompted by the Holy Spirit at work inside of her.

The legendary woman is also a picture of meekness, but that meekness should never be mistaken for weakness. Her meekness is the power God has given her, submitted to the control of the Holy Spirit. You are likely familiar with the Beatitude that says, "Blessed are the meek, for they shall inherit the earth" (Matt. 5:5). The Greek word translated "meek" is *praus*, and it is generally understood to mean mild, humble, or meek.[1] But there is much more to the meaning of that word. *Praus* was also used by the ancient Greeks to describe war horses. For example, Xenophon used the word several times in *On the Art of Horsemanship*.[2] When the Greeks were training horses for battle, they did not want weak horses. They wanted powerful horses, but they needed that power to be under control so it could be used wisely and effectively. A horse whose power and strength could not be tamed and controlled was of no use in battle. When soldiers were training horses, they needed high-spirited horses that could be "kept in check."[3]

The meekness of the legendary woman is much the same, except instead of being under the control of a soldier, she is submitted to the will of her heavenly Father. She keeps her strength and power in check, making her wise and effective in battle. She takes her orders from the Lord, and she executes them with accuracy. When God says move, she moves. When He says to stay put, she stays put. She wants to be an effective warrior for the King of kings, so she puts on meekness like a garment. She is strong enough to stay silent when only action is needed. She is humble enough to act in stealth and secrecy at the command of her Lord. She keeps her strength and power in check until it is time to use it to fulfill her calling and advance the kingdom of God. She is not afraid to go into battle, because she knows the source of her strength.

Disobedience and rebellion can be hindrances to the stealthy warrior since a warrior needs to obey orders. But laziness is also a hindrance. Soldiers train for battle, and they train hard. Their training protects them and enables them to act with confidence. If soldiers are lazy and are not diligent about their training, they put themselves and others at risk and jeopardize the success of their missions. The legendary woman must be diligent to develop her skills and strengthen herself in the Lord so she is ready when her moment to take action comes.

Another hindrance to the stealthy warrior is battle fatigue. If a legendary woman relies on her own strength in battle, she will quickly "grow weary while doing good" (Gal. 6:9). That is why the legendary woman must always remember that the Lord is her strength, and the battle belongs to Him (Exod. 15:2; 1 Sam. 17:47). She counts on the Lord to renew her strength and restore her soul, and she knows that whatever she does in secret, God will reward openly.

Legendary women face all kinds of battles, both physical and spiritual, and often those battles require actions rather than words to defeat the enemy. The legendary woman always remembers who her enemy really is. The enemy may be disguised as flesh and blood, but the legendary woman knows the true battle is "against principalities, against powers, against the rulers of the darkness of this age, against spiritual hosts of wickedness in the heavenly places" (Eph. 6:12).

POWER IN THE HAND OF A WOMAN

During the time of the judges, when the prophetess Deborah was the judge over Israel, it was a difficult time for the children of Israel. They had been "harshly oppressed" by Jabin, the king of Hazor, for twenty years (Judg. 4:3). Sisera was the commander of Jabin's army and therefore the primary oppressor of the people. Deborah heard from the Lord that the men of Israel were to go into battle against Sisera and the Canaanite army because the Lord was going to deliver Sisera into their hands. But the Lord also told Deborah that there would be no glory for the men of Israel because the Lord would "sell Sisera into the hand of a woman" (Judg. 4:9).

That woman was named Jael. She was a homemaker, a stay-at-home mom. And the battle between Israel and the armies of Jabin came right to her front door when Sisera showed up in need of a safe hiding place. This Kenite woman stepped right up into the role of a legendary woman. She knew who Sisera was. She knew of his arrogance, his cruelty, his oppression, and his brutality, and she knew what he would do to her if she were numbered among the tribes and peoples he had defeated and subdued. And she knew it wasn't the time to talk; it was the time for action. She didn't go to her next-door neighbor to get her opinion on what she should do about the army commander asleep in her home. She acted, and she took out the enemy with stealth.

Legendary woman, you will face times when you need to be a stealthy warrior. You will need to act in obedience to the command of the Lord to take out the enemy. Words will not be needed, just the strength of character to obey and act.

Jael lived in a tent. Deborah said of her, "Most blessed among women is Jael, the wife of Heber the Kenite; blessed is she among women in tents" (Judg. 5:24). During that time period, everything related to pitching the tent would have been the responsibility of a woman, so Jael had plenty of practice at putting up the tent, getting it properly tied down, and driving the tent pegs into the ground to keep the tent secure. So when Sisera fell asleep in the tent, she used skills she already possessed and items she had at hand to do an amazing exploit:

> Then Jael, Heber's wife, took a tent peg and took a hammer in her hand, and went softly to him and drove

the peg into his temple, and it went down into the
ground; for he was fast asleep and weary. So he died.

—JUDGES 4:21

She killed the commander of the army by driving a tent peg.
She didn't make a big production of it. She didn't shout out her
intention for all to hear. She just did what she was called to do.
Even when Barak came looking for Sisera, she didn't play the
part of the drama queen, relating all the details of what had
occurred before she brought him into the tent to see Sisera. She
simply said, "Come, I will show you the man whom you seek"
(Judg. 4:22).

Jael was in the correct position to deliver a deadly blow to
the enemy. So when the opportunity presented itself, she took
it, like the legendary woman she was. Jael was in the right
place at the right time, armed with the right weapon. God
used a homemaker to take out a strongman, and God can use
you the same way. When the opportunity presents itself for
you to defeat the enemy, use whatever skills and tools you have
at hand to take him out. The Lord is your strength, and He
will put you in the right place at the right time with the right
weapon.

There was another legendary woman who faced similar circumstances. There was a wicked man named Abimelech who
killed sixty-nine of his seventy brothers so he could rule over
Israel. (See Judges 9.) Three years later the men of Shechem,
who had supported Abimelech's seizure of power and con-
spired with him to kill his brothers, rose up against him in a
clear case of reaping what you sow. Abimelech went to battle
against Shechem, demolishing the city and salting the land.
The survivors holed up together in a stronghold, but Abimelech
set fire to it, burning alive about a thousand men and women.
He then turned his sights toward Thebez, and once again the
people fled to a stronghold, a tower. Abimelech had the same

plan to set fire to the tower and burn the people alive. But then a legendary woman stepped up.

We don't even know her name. The Bible just refers to her as "a certain woman" (Judg. 9:53). But as Abimelech drew near the door of the tower, she dropped a millstone on his head, crushing his skull and ending his diabolical reign over Israel. Once again, a woman was in the right place at the right time, armed with the right weapon. She used the strength she already possessed from her labors, and she used an item she had at hand to do an amazing exploit. She didn't say a word. She just acted to protect herself and others. She took out the enemy with stealth and accuracy. And though we may not know her name, God knows her name, and her actions taken for the protection of others were pleasing in His sight.

The same is true of you, legendary woman. When you use the strengths God has been developing in you to protect yourself and others—whether physically or spiritually—your actions are pleasing in His sight. We live in a world where we encounter people in need of defense and protection on a regular basis. God has given you unique skills and abilities to be a warrior for Him, to be His hands and feet in an ongoing battle to protect those He loves. It is time for you to rise up, arm yourself with your God-given skills and abilities, and be the stealthy warrior God has called you to be.

YOUR DEFINING MOMENT

For both Jael and the "certain woman," their defining moments as stealthy warriors came when they used the wisdom, strength, and skills they already possessed to defeat the enemy. They didn't need the spotlight. They didn't need a fanfare or a standing ovation. They didn't need to make lofty speeches, drawing attention to their actions. They just did what needed to be done to take out their enemies.

Another legendary woman who labored mostly in silence

to defeat the enemy was Harriet Tubman. She escaped from slavery and then became a conductor on the Underground Railroad, leading about twenty missions to rescue people from slavery. She also worked as a spy during the Civil War, contributing to the rescue of countless others. In a letter to Harriet, fellow abolitionist Frederick Douglass wrote:

> The difference between us is very marked. Most that I have done and suffered in the service of our cause has been in public, and I have received much encouragement at every step of the way. You on the other hand have labored in a private way. I have wrought in the day— you in the night. I have had the applause of the crowd and the satisfaction that comes of being approved by the multitude, while the most that you have done has been witnessed by a few trembling, scarred, and foot-sore bondmen and women, whom you have led out of the house of bondage, and whose heartfelt "God bless you" has been your only reward. The midnight sky and the silent stars have been the witnesses of your devotion to freedom and of your heroism.[4]

Although Harriet Tubman is famous for her exploits today, Douglass' letter reveals that much of her work was done behind the scenes, silently and quietly, with few other than the Lord to take notice at first. She worked in the dark to fulfill her calling. And her silence and lack of recognition was at times her protector. For example, one time she sat silently in a train car as a poster offering a twelve-thousand-dollar reward for her capture was put up over her head.[5]

Don't get discouraged if you find yourself behind the scenes, out of the spotlight, or flying under the radar. Remember that the Lord will reward openly what you do in secret. There are times when the Lord will keep you hidden for your protection.

He isn't finished with you yet, and He doesn't want anything to hinder His plans for you.

Harriet Tubman continued trusting the Lord to protect her: "she had her duty to perform, and she expected to be taken care of till it was done."[6] And even after she gained some notoriety, she often let her actions do the talking. On her way to an anti-slavery meeting in 1860, she learned of a fugitive slave who had been captured and was going to be taken back to the South. She headed straight for the US Commissioner's office, where the man was being detained, and a crowd followed in her wake. She marched up and planted herself on the stairs in front of the door. Her presence there alerted others that the man was still there, and the crowd continued to grow. When the officers tried to make her move, she stood her ground with her head down and her arms folded. She didn't say a word; she didn't have to. She was a picture of meekness. She was a stealthy warrior.

Harriet knew she was strong, and she knew she had the crowd behind her, but it wasn't the right moment yet. So she waited, silently and meekly. And when the right moment came, she used what she had at hand. When the officers brought the man out, she called out to the crowd, "Here he comes—take him!" In the ensuing chaos, she wrapped her arms around the slave, and they were knocked to the ground together. Harriet used what she had at hand—the sunbonnet off her head—to disguise the slave, enabling her to get him to a boat on the river. While it wasn't all smooth sailing from there, the slave did end up escaping safely to Canada.[7] Legendary woman, God wants you to be a warrior who sets people free.

Harriet Tubman was a legendary woman of fiery faith, amazing courage, extravagant giving, keen discernment, and fierce love. She was also a stealthy warrior, one who was willing to follow the orders of her Lord. Her meekness and humility made her a secret weapon in the hands of a God who wants to defeat the enemy and set people free. Her defining moment was when she chose to wait for the right moment, even when the officers were pushing her to give up and the crowd was pushing her to charge headlong into the battle. And then when the right moment came, she acted, using her God-given skills and whatever she had at hand. And the result was freedom.

As a legendary woman, your defining moment will come when God puts you at the right place at the right time, armed with the right weapon. And that weapon will be a skill you already possess or something you have at hand. You won't be hindered by disobedience, rebellion, laziness, lack of training, or battle fatigue. God doesn't need weapons of mass destruction to destroy the enemy; He just needs diligent, willing warriors who will follow orders. God will use women who can be content to stay silent and in the background until their moments come. He wants legendary women who have put on meekness like a garment and will await His command to move. And when He says move, they will move. They will take action. They will head into battle, determined to defeat the enemy of their souls by whatever means they can. They will do heroic exploits for the glory of the Lord.

The legendary woman isn't necessarily physically strong, although she might be; rather, she is spiritually strong. The Lord is her strength (Exod. 15:2). She seeks the Lord and His strength (1 Chron. 16:11). She calls upon the Lord, saying, "O my strength, haste thee to help me" (Ps. 22:19, kjv). She knows that "those who wait on the LORD shall renew their strength" (Isa. 40:31).

It's interesting that the word translated "strength" in Psalm 22:19 traces back to a root word that means to twist.[8] Isaiah 40:31 uses a different word for *strength*, but the word it uses for *wait* means to bind or twist together.[9] I think this is a key part of the legendary woman's preparation for her defining moment. She gains her needed strength by being bound together with the

Lord. She looks to Him, she waits on Him, and she is strengthened by Him when she spends time with Him. And that binding together, that twisting, is her strength. And that strength gives her the ability to do whatever is needed to defeat the enemy.

The legendary woman's strength and meekness is also her legacy. She may never receive credit on the world stage for her successful missions. The only ones who know of her exploits may be the few she rescued and her Father in heaven. The world may never know her name, but God knows her name. He sees her and the things she does. And the only accolade the legendary woman truly needs is to hear the Lord say, "Well done, good and faithful servant." She may have used unconventional methods to deliver her family, her community, her nation, or even the world, but it was the power of God working behind those unconventional methods that brought success. And if people do notice that her mission was successful, they will want to know where her strength comes from. And in that moment she need no longer be silent; she can open up her mouth and give all the glory to God, the One who gives her strength.

PRAYER TO BECOME A STEALTHY WARRIOR

Lord, make me a stealthy warrior for You. Give me strength and wisdom to follow Your orders. You are my strength and my defense. Grant me meekness that I may be effective in battle. Deliver me from any spirits of rebellion or laziness. Help me to develop the skills You have given me so I am ready to defeat the enemy when the time comes. Lord, I submit to Your will. I will move when You say move and stay still when You say stay still. I will act to protect others. I will act to set people free. I am a doer of Your Word. Let me not grow weary in doing good. Reward openly what I do in secret. May my actions be pleasing in Your sight.

DECLARATIONS TO AWAKEN THE WARRIOR WITHIN

I am a warrior for the Lord.

I am God's secret weapon.

I obey the orders of my commander.

I am a doer of the Word.

I am meek, but I am not weak.

I am submitted to the will of God.

The Lord is my strength.

I seek the Lord and His strength.

I wait upon the Lord and renew my strength.

I am bound together with the Lord.

God sees me and knows my name.

I am not disobedient or rebellious.

I train diligently and am not hindered by laziness.

I do not grow weary in doing good.

God will reward openly what I do in secret.

I take out the enemy at the command of the Lord.

I use my skills and whatever I have at hand to do amazing exploits.

I will be in the right place at the right time with the right weapon.

Chapter 11

IN PURSUIT OF PURPOSE

Legendary Women Are Destiny Driven

We are made for larger ends than *earth* can compass.
Oh, let us be true to our exalted destiny.

—CATHERINE BOOTH

T HE LEGENDARY WOMAN is destiny driven. She knows she has a purpose, and she pursues it wholeheartedly. She knows she has a unique and wonderful place in this world, and she celebrates that and makes her place in the world known. Because she is driven to fulfill her God-given purpose, she never second-guesses her value, and it's not easy for others to do it either. She is industrious, creative, consistent, focused, and filled with ingenuity as she labors to complete her mission for the Lord. She has found her niche, the place where she can use her gifts and talents for the glory of God, and she knows where she belongs because her destiny propels her forward.

The legendary woman understands that "to everything there is a season, a time for every purpose under heaven" (Eccles. 3:1). She knows that this is her season, her time of purpose and destiny. And she understands the value of her God-given purpose. The Hebrew word translated "purpose" in that verse is *ḥēpeṣ*, and it means pleasure, a valuable thing, or something precious.[1] The legendary woman knows that her purpose, her destiny, is something precious; it has great value, and it brings pleasure both to her and to the heart of God. So she pursues her purpose with all that she has. She has "purpose of heart" (Acts 11:23).

The legendary woman's purpose, her destiny, is no ordinary thing. She has been "called...with a holy calling" (2 Tim. 1:9). The word translated "called" in that verse is *kaleō*. It means to call, invite, to be called to bear a name or title, to call forth.[2] And the word translated "calling," *klēsis*, means calling, vocation, invitation; the divine invitation to embrace the salvation of God.[3] As a legendary woman, you were not set free from your sin, your past, your shame, your chains, your bondage, and all those other things merely for the sake of freedom. When Jesus freed you, He called you to bear the title of daughter of the Most High, one of His own special people. He called you forth from darkness into His marvelous light, and He called you to be a light to those still in darkness. It is your holy calling, your vocation. You were issued a divine invitation to walk in freedom and to help others walk in it too. Your calling is sacred.

Don't be hindered by the lies of the enemy. He will try to tell you that there really isn't a purpose for your life, that your life has no meaning, that you have no value, that everything that happens is just random chance. None of that is true. The Book of Psalms says:

> Your eyes saw my substance, being yet unformed. And in Your book they all were written, the days fashioned for me, when as yet there were none of them.
> —PSALM 139:16

That means that even before you were born, God had a plan and a purpose for your life. You are not an accident. You have value. Your life has meaning. You were not born into this world at this time by chance. You have a purpose, a divine purpose, an assignment from heaven designed specifically for you. Don't let the enemy distract you from that purpose with his lies.

THE SEED OF DESTINY

Your destiny, your divine purpose, begins with a small seed planted in your heart by the Lord Most High. The Word says, "He has also planted eternity [a sense of divine purpose] in the human heart [a mysterious longing which nothing under the sun can satisfy, except God]" (Eccles. 3:11, AMP). The only way you can truly fill that longing for a sense of divine purpose is to know and pursue your divine purpose. You can do a million good and godly things, but if they are not part of your purpose, they will only bring temporary satisfaction at best. You must have the courage to say no to things that are not part of your assignment.

God planted that seed of divine destiny in your heart, but you need to cultivate it so it can grow.

Just like natural seeds, what God has planted in you needs water:

> "He who believes in Me, as the Scripture has said, out of his heart will flow rivers of living water." But this He spoke concerning the Spirit, whom those believing in Him would receive.
>
> —JOHN 7:38–39

> Christ also loved the church and gave Himself for her, that He might sanctify and cleanse her with the washing of water by the word.
>
> —EPHESIANS 5:25–26

> But the water that I shall give him will become in him a fountain of water springing up into everlasting life.
>
> —JOHN 4:14

What God has planted in you needs light:

> The Lord is my light and my salvation.
>
> —Psalm 27:1

> Your word is a lamp to my feet and a light to my path.
>
> —Psalm 119:105

What God has planted in you needs to be nourished:

> Your words were found, and I ate them, and Your word was to me the joy and rejoicing of my heart.
>
> —Jeremiah 15:16

> As newborn babes, desire the pure milk of the word, that you may grow thereby, if indeed you have tasted that the Lord is gracious.
>
> —1 Peter 2:2–3

> I am the vine, you are the branches. He who abides in Me, and I in him, bears much fruit; for without Me you can do nothing.
>
> —John 15:5

And once the seed has grown, it needs to be pruned:

> I am the true vine, and My Father is the vinedresser. Every branch in Me that does not bear fruit He takes away; and every branch that bears fruit He prunes, that it may bear more fruit.
>
> —John 15:1–2

The Lord wants you to be fruitful. He wants you to do more than just talk about your destiny; He wants you to act. When God makes you free, you are free indeed (John 8:36). That means you are free of excuses—no more limitations or obstacles based on your gender, color, social class, or economic status. A legendary woman in pursuit of her purpose does not fall victim to any mentality that provides an excuse or a limitation or a false expectation or a barrier.

Knowing your God-given purpose emboldens you to face down the opposition. You know who you are because you know whose you are, and nothing is going to stand in the way of your pursuit of your purpose. Knowing your purpose lessens your options because you realize God's way is the only path. Your destiny will keep you alive. Your destiny will give you strength to be single minded. Destiny is like oxygen in your lungs; it keeps you breathing. It gives you a reason to get out of bed.

PURSUING DIVINE PURPOSE

Ruth was a biblical legendary woman who was destiny driven. She pursued her divine purpose. She faced many hardships, among them poverty and being widowed at a young age. The odds were stacked against her, but she did not stay in a place of brokenness.

Ruth's story begins with a man named Elimelech, who left the land of Canaan for Moab during a time of famine. But the famine was a time of judgment against Israel for violating the covenant God had established with them. (See Leviticus 26:18–20.) Elimelech's choice may have been wise according to worldly wisdom, but it was anything but wise according to spiritual wisdom because you can't outrun the Lord's judgments. Many times they are the consequences of our own sin, and they are also a sign that God loves us, "for whom the LORD loves He chastens" (Heb. 12:6).

While Elimelech's family may have temporarily escaped the famine, they actually ended up worse off than they would have been if they had stayed in Bethlehem—Elimelech and both his sons died in Moab. After their deaths, Elimelech's widow, Naomi, decided to return to her homeland. She had two Moabite daughters-in-law, Ruth and Orpah, and she urged them to return to their own families. Orpah relented and left, but Ruth clung to her mother-in-law, and in her defining moment when she set out in pursuit of her destiny, she eloquently spoke of her determination to go with her:

> Entreat me not to leave you, or to turn back from following after you; for wherever you go, I will go; and wherever you lodge, I will lodge; your people shall be my people, and your God, my God. Where you die, I will die, and there will I be buried. The LORD do so to me, and more also, if anything but death parts you and me.
>
> —RUTH 1:16–17

Even though Ruth was born into a culture that neither knew nor worshipped the Lord, her marriage to an Israelite had introduced her to the one true God. And even in the short time she was married, she saw and learned enough to know that the Lord was the real deal, not an idol made by human hands. She also knew that her destiny did not lie in Moab, and that knowledge compelled her to step out in faith, to take a risk, to venture to an unknown land. She had a destiny and a purpose to pursue, and she couldn't do that if she stayed in Moab. And she wasn't going to let any social or cultural barriers stand in her way.

Legendary woman, you cannot let social or cultural barriers stand in your way either. We live in a time when people are divided along so many lines that it is hard to keep track of them all. But God is no respecter of persons; He shows no partiality (Acts 10:34). We are all one in Christ Jesus (Gal. 3:28). Don't let social or cultural differences prevent you from pursuing your divine purpose.

When Ruth declared her commitment to Naomi, she was making a covenant not only with Naomi but also with the Lord. Ruth made herself a willing vessel, ready for the Lord to fill. She made herself available for God to cultivate the seed of destiny within her and prune away anything that might be standing in the way of its fulfillment. And because of Ruth's willingness and her trust in the Lord, God directed her paths. She returned to Bethlehem with Naomi and ended up marrying a kinsman redeemer named Boaz. And as a result, she was the great-grandmother of King David and one of the few women named in the genealogy of Jesus in Matthew 1. By discovering and pursuing her destiny, Ruth played a role in the coming of the Messiah.

YOUR DEFINING MOMENT

As a destiny-driven legendary woman, your defining moment will come when you discover your God-given purpose, your destiny, and make the choice to pursue it with all that you have and all that you are. And while the end result may not always be known at the beginning, you trust God wholeheartedly, knowing that His plan for you is a good one and He will direct your paths. Your defining moment comes when you realize that you are on this earth with an assignment from heaven. Legendary women must know that God does all things on purpose. He makes all things work together for good to those who are called according to His purpose (Rom. 8:28). If you are not in purpose, you are in perversion.

When you are in your assignment, you have a sense of urgency. The Holy Spirit of God drives you, which is where the urgency comes from. God starts to lead and guide you to do the simple things of the gospel. Then He begins to unfold, reveal, and give you insight into the greater things. Legendary woman, God will take you from glory to glory, assignment to assignment. You must understand that you are prewired for the work He has called you to. Before He formed you in your mother's belly, He knew you. Your days were fashioned in a book of destiny before you were in the earth. The legendary woman's life's quest is to live her days according to this book.

She shifts seasons and moves throughout life with heaven's master plan for her life.

Your defining moment may often mean a complete change in direction, but it is always worth it. That's because while the end result here on earth may not always be clear, you are also aiming for the heavenly end result of hearing, "Well done, good and faithful servant."

For Bible teacher and legendary woman Joyce Meyer, I believe her defining moment occurred in her car in 1976. A survivor of childhood sexual abuse, Meyer was born again at the age of nine. As she describes it, "Although I was born of the Spirit, I never knew it. I had no teaching on that subject, and therefore I remained in darkness experientially even though the Light was living in me....I struggled for many years."[4] Fast-forward to 1976. She was in her car on the way to work and was feeling discouraged, frustrated, and desperate. She cried out to the Lord, saying, "God, something is missing."[5] She was spiritually hungry and open to whatever God wanted to do. And she heard God call her name. She knew "with certainty that God was going to do something...He was about to move in [her] life."[6] The Holy Spirit filled her in a way she had never experienced before, and she was changed. God promises that when you seek Him with your whole heart, you find Him (Jer. 29:13), and that is what happened to Joyce.

God was calling Joyce to change the trajectory of her life and step into her destiny. And she was a willing vessel. But as often happens when we begin to passionately pursue our purpose, the enemy stepped in to try and defeat her. She faced rejection and disapproval on multiple fronts. Satan tempted her to forget what God had done and just go back to being "normal."

But I knew that God had done something wonderful in my life. I had never felt like that before, and I made the decision that even if I never had any friends, I could not go back to what I used to be and have. It was not satisfying them, and it would never be.

I simply had to go on with God no matter what the cost![7]

Within three weeks of Joyce's baptism with the Holy Spirit, God directed her to begin teaching a Bible study, and more than forty years later she is still faithfully teaching the Word.

Like all legendary women, both Ruth and Joyce Meyer faced moments of decision. God was calling them by name, opening their hearts and minds to discover His planned destiny for them. And they both had the opportunity to go back to the way things used to be, to the familiar, to the comfortable, to the path of least resistance. But they both chose to pursue their purpose and work toward fulfilling their God-given callings. They did not let any obstacles get in their way.

As I have said before, destiny is not decided; it is discovered. You need to be a willing vessel who says, "Lord, show me Your purpose for my life." You need to lay down your dreams and desires for yourself and pick up the ones God has for you, knowing that when you "delight yourself also in the LORD... He shall give you the desires of your heart" (Ps. 37:4). As Joyce Meyer wrote, "To be filled with the Holy Spirit means to live our life for God's glory and pleasure, not for our own. It means laying down the life we had planned and discovering and following His plan for us."[8]

Legendary woman, when you are destiny driven, you do not waste time on unfruitful things. You will be a vine that bears much fruit. This is your time; this is your season. Your calling is a holy invitation from the Lord Most High to walk in His ways and do mighty works for the advancement of His kingdom on earth. It is your opportunity to cultivate the seed of destiny planted in your heart.

While it is true that it is a great thing for a legendary woman to discover her destiny early in life, it doesn't mean that your life has been a waste if you have yet to discover yours. Remember that "all things work together for good to those who love God, to those who are the called according to His purpose" (Rom. 8:28). God doesn't waste your life experiences. If a woman discovers her destiny and purpose later in life, God has shown Himself faithful in redeeming her time and restoring her years.

If you have already experienced your defining moment of destiny as a legendary woman, praise the Lord! Keep pursuing His path for your life without letting any obstacles get in your way. Keep your eyes fixed on Jesus, the author and finisher of your faith. Stay focused and stay willing. Leave a legacy of fiery faith, fierce love, and great courage as you fulfill your God-given destiny. The Lord has already walked through your life, and everything is finished in Him. He has already written your story. He has sent the Holy Spirit to guide your life each day with daily bread. Jesus will become the power of His own purpose. Jesus is the way, but the heart of the Father for your life is the destination! There is a full-grown Jesus inside of you. Legendary woman, you are being guided. It is when you submit to this process that you receive direction and instruction and experience miracles and the supernatural.

If you haven't experienced your defining moment yet, get ready! Prepare yourself body, soul, and spirit to be a willing vessel. Everyone has a book of destiny. Your days were fashioned for you before there were any (Ps. 139:16). God has ordered and predetermined your days. Delight yourself in the Lord. Ask Him to show you His plan and purpose for your life. God will help you find your wonderful place, the place where you can use the gifts and talents He has given you to walk toward your destiny. And when He shows you, step into your destiny with faith, courage, and obedience, trusting the Lord to help you overcome any excuses and any obstacles. Your assignment will give you access to revelation. You are a legendary woman, and with God all things are possible.

PRAYER TO WALK IN PURPOSE

God, I thank You that You have already written my story. I thank You that I am prewired for success. You've sent me into the earth with everything I need to fulfill Your purpose through me. Lord, I ask You to reveal to me every day the meaning of my life. Holy Spirit, I ask that You guide me through life with daily bread. God, You are the One writing my story, and You will make all things work together for my good. I want to live every day moving toward my purpose. Lord, fill me with the knowledge of Your will. Let me have wisdom and spiritual understanding. I want to walk worthy of You.

DECLARATIONS FOR PURSUING YOUR PURPOSE

I have an assignment from heaven.

God is writing my story, and He will make all things work together for me.

I have a purpose. I am not in the world by chance. I am not in this decade by chance.

I have value.

I have meaning.

I was born for the times.

I have a full-grown Jesus living inside of me.

I will yield to the leadings of the Holy Spirit.

My destiny is sure and complete in Christ.

I am anointed for my assignment.

I will finish my work with joy.

I will not be stagnant, but I will shift with every season of my destiny.

I will not hesitate.

I will not waste time on things I'm not called to.

I have courage to say no to things that are not part of my assignment.

I will be a woman of revelation.

I will be a woman who walks by faith.

I will discern the grace of God upon my life.

I will serve with and by grace.

Lord, continue to release the grace and anointing to fulfill my assignment.

I will stay in my measure of rule.

Chapter 12

PUSHING THROUGH AND PRESSING ON

Legendary Women Have an Overcomer's Heart

Don't quit, and don't give up. The reward is just around
the corner. And in times of doubt or times of joy, listen
for that still, small voice. Know that God has been
there from the beginning—and he will be there until...
The End.

—JOANNA GAINES

THE LEGENDARY WOMAN possesses the heart of an over-comer. Push through, press on, stay the course, stick with it, remain, don't give up, don't grow weary, keep going a little further, you can make it, you can do it, get back up, don't stop, never give up, pursue, overtake, recover—these are the words the legendary woman hears in her mind and heart in the midst of life's most difficult seasons. She closes her eyes, takes a deep breath, and reminds herself to never ever give up. She is a child of God, she was called with a purpose, and all things are possible with God.

"Life is hard, but God is good" is not a tired cliché to ignore. It is reality. It is truth. The legendary woman does not lose heart, because she has seen the goodness of the Lord in the land of the living (Ps. 27:13). She knows the Lord is "abounding in goodness" (Exod. 34:6) because she has seen the evidence in her own life, even during trying times. She knows that good-ness and mercy will follow her all the days of her life (Ps. 23:6).

Therefore, the legendary woman is an overcomer. She knows that no matter what she faces, Jesus has overcome the world (John 16:33). And because the legendary woman has been born of God, she overcomes the world too. Her victory that overcomes the world is her faith (1 John 5:4). The Greek word for *overcome* is *nikaō*. It means to conquer, to carry off the victory, to get the victory, to subdue, to overcome, to deprive of power to harm, to prevail, to win.[1] Because of her position in Christ, the legendary woman has been positioned to be victorious, to win, to prevail, and to conquer. In fact through Christ she is more than a conqueror (Rom. 8:37). And the word translated "more than conquerors" in Romans 8 is *hypernikaō*, a compound word formed from *nikaō*, which we just defined, and *hyper*, meaning over, above, beyond, exceedingly above, abundantly above.[2] The legendary woman has been equipped to go over and exceedingly above in her victory.

Knowing that her victory is guaranteed, the legendary woman runs her race of faith with endurance, laying aside every weight and the sin that so easily ensnares her (Heb. 12:1). She holds on and keeps her hands on the plow until her job or assignment is completed. She will stop at nothing to accomplish the mission God has given her. She wears the mantle God has placed upon her with joy, and she will not let anything make her cast it off.

The legendary woman also knows the keys to overcoming. She keeps her eyes fixed on Jesus. She understands that everything He has spoken is true. He doesn't just speak truth; He is the truth! She endures. She prays. She reads the Word. She is patient. She has faith. She proclaims the truth. She trusts God to keep His promises. She spends time in the presence of God. And she remembers that it is God who gives her victory through her Lord Jesus Christ (1 Cor. 15:57).

FOCUS ON THE PROMISE

Our biblical example of a legendary woman with an overcomer's heart is Hannah. Hannah was barren. She faced month after month and year after year without the child her heart longed for. And on top of her barrenness, she had to face her rival, Peninnah, who provoked her endlessly, making Hannah even more miserable. But Hannah had hope in her heart. She had endurance. She had faith. She spent time in the presence of God. And she prayed:

> O LORD of hosts, if You will indeed look on the afflic-
> tion of Your maidservant and remember me, and not
> forget Your maidservant, but will give Your maidservant
> a male child, then I will give him to the LORD all the
> days of his life, and no razor shall come upon his head.
> —1 SAMUEL 1:11

One of the meanings of Hannah's name is prayer.[3] Living up to her name was a vital part of Hannah's path to victory, to overcoming. The Word says, "The effective, fervent prayer of a righteous man [or woman] avails much" (Jas. 5:16). And that certainly was the case with Hannah. She "prayed to the LORD and wept in anguish" and "poured out [her] soul before the LORD" (1 Sam. 1:10, 15). She was so fervent as she prayed to the Lord that the priest thought she was drunk. Hannah explained the truth to the priest, and he said, "Go in peace, and the God of Israel grant your petition which you have asked of Him" (v. 17). Then Hannah went away with a heart full of hope rather than despair. And I believe that was her defining moment. She had endured much, persisted in prayer, and maintained her faith, and she believed she was finally going to overcome. Hannah soon conceived and then gave birth to a son, whom she named Samuel, meaning "heard of God," a testimony to her answered prayer.[4] The legendary woman knows that God hears her, so she persists in prayer. She does not give up until the plans and purposes of God are conceived and brought to fulfillment in her life.

Hannah left a powerful legacy for other legendary women. She demonstrated how to endure and stay focused on the promise of God for your life, a key to making it through those times and seasons when it seems as if nothing is changing, growing, or moving forward. Hannah was an example of how to overcome the temptation to compromise and settle for less than God's best for you as well as how to overcome ungodly criticism and judgment from others. She persisted in prayer, even though the answer to her prayer seemed to take years. She understood that sometimes the vision God has given us seems to tarry, but we need to wait for the appointed time (Hab. 2:3).

Hannah had been chosen by God to be the mother of Samuel, a great prophet of whom it was said, "The LORD was with him and let none of his words fall to the ground" (1 Sam. 3:19). But there was a time of preparation for Hannah, and the preparation time can be frightening because you are in the dark about what God is doing. It is a time when your trust is challenged. But the legendary woman knows that even when she doesn't understand the workings of the Lord's hand, she can trust His love for her.

Hannah possessed an overcomer's heart. She had great faith that carried her through her desert season, her barren season. The testing of her faith produced patience and endurance (Jas. 1:3). She developed the victory to overcome the world through her faith (1 John 5:4).

ANYWAY

On the wall of Mother Teresa's children's home in Calcutta there is a sign with the Paradoxical Commandments, written by Kent M. Keith. Even though Mother Teresa didn't write the commandments, they resonated strongly enough with her that she chose to have them enlarged and posted on a sign as a powerful reminder:

> People are unreasonable, illogical, and
> self-centered,

LOVE THEM ANYWAY
If you do good, people will accuse you of selfish, ulterior motives,
DO GOOD ANYWAY
If you are successful, you win false friends and true enemies,
SUCCEED ANYWAY
The good you do will be forgotten tomorrow,
DO GOOD ANYWAY
Honesty and frankness make you vulnerable,
BE HONEST AND FRANK ANYWAY
What you spent years building may be destroyed overnight,
BUILD ANYWAY
People really need help but may attack you if you help them,
HELP PEOPLE ANYWAY
Give the world the best you have and you'll get kicked in the teeth,
GIVE THE WORLD THE BEST YOU'VE GOT ANYWAY.[5]

This captures the overcoming heart of the legendary woman. The enemy is going to throw everything he can at you to prevent you from fulfilling the calling of God for your life. But as a legendary woman, you can't let the enemy stop you. He may stir up fear in your heart; be courageous anyway. He may try to fill your heart with hate, bitterness, and callousness; be filled with fierce love and driving compassion anyway. He may plant doubt in your mind and your heart; have fiery faith anyway. He may tempt you to go your own way, to do whatever feels "right" to you or is easy, or to disobey what God is telling you to do; be obedient anyway. He may try to make you think that confronting injustice and being an advocate for yourself and others is unfeminine or useless; be confrontational anyway.

The enemy may make you think you are foolish, stupid, and blind; be wise and discerning anyway. He may try to convince you that you have little or no value and that negotiating on behalf of yourself or others is pointless; be a master negotiator anyway. He may prompt you to be selfish and hoard whatever you have; be an extravagant giver anyway. He may tempt you to sit around and gossip about a problem rather than taking action to fix it; be a stealthy warrior anyway. He may tempt you to worship anything and everything other than God and to be selfish instead of sacrificial; pour yourself out anyway. The enemy may try to convince you that you have no purpose and that God would never bother with someone like you; be destiny driven anyway. He may tell you that you can never win; overcome anyway.

The legendary woman pushes forward, no matter what obstacles the enemy throws in her path. She pursues, she overtakes, and she recovers what the enemy has stolen from her. She is an overcomer, and God gives her the victory through her Lord Jesus Christ (1 Cor. 15:57).

The legendary woman has no qualms about showing the enemy what she is made of. I will say it again: when you know whose you are, you know who you are. Your identity comes from what God says about you. You are forgiven. You are redeemed. You are beautiful. You are fearfully and wonderfully made. You are accepted. You have been chosen. You are a daughter of the Most High God. You have access to the throne of grace. You are special. You have been called with a purpose. When the enemy attacks you with a lie, fight back with truth. And remember, "No weapon formed against you shall prosper, and every tongue which rises against you in judgment you shall condemn. This is the heritage of the servants of the Lord, and their righteousness is from Me,' says the Lord" (Isa. 54:17).

Legendary woman and Bible teacher Beth Moore has an overcomer's heart. She was a victim of childhood sexual abuse. Even while pursuing God's purpose and plan for her life, she was hiding her own brokenness. Her defining moment of overcoming came when she decided to break free from her brokenness instead of carrying it around as a heavy burden. She put her past behind her by using the truth of God's Word. She said, "I would memorize scripture. I put those truths on index cards and I would take those things with me everywhere I went. I would walk around the grocery store...I was just saying those scriptures over and over."[6]

And Beth Moore has used her platform as a renowned Bible teacher and author to be an advocate for sexual abuse survivors and to inspire others to be overcomers as well. It is part of her legacy as a legendary woman. In December 2019 she tweeted:

> This culture's training us to be fragile. To be sure, there are things worthy of offense, worthy of calling out, but we're being shaped societally to be wounded, hurt and offended constantly. This is antithetical to the commission of Christ. We're called to be strong in the Lord. We are called to be the ones who, like those earliest Jesus-followers, get beaten up and keep getting back up. We are called to carry crosses, not grudges. We're called to spiritual tenacity. Fierce love. Fiery faith. If you want to be mad all the time, let the world train you. But, if you want to have an iota of joy in this offended world & save your energy for the things that really are worth being hurt by, get back into the strength training worthy of New Testament saints. We are not wimps. We are warriors in a battle against the powers of darkness.[7]

And Beth Moore practices what she preaches. When John MacArthur commented that she should "go home"—simply because she is a woman who teaches the Word—she didn't play the victim. She didn't hold a grudge. She didn't call him names. She tweeted:

> I did not surrender to a calling of man when I was 18 years old. I surrendered to a calling of God. It never occurs to me for a second to not fulfill it. I will follow Jesus—and Jesus alone—all the way home. And I will see His beautiful face and proclaim, Worthy is the Lamb! Here's the beautiful thing about it & I mean this with absolute respect. You don't have to let me serve you. That gets to be your choice. Whether or not I serve Jesus is not up to you. Whether I serve you certainly is. One way or the other, I esteem you as my sibling in Christ.[8]

She chose to show grace. She chose to esteem a man as her brother in Christ. And she chose to not let anything get in the way of her calling from God. This is the choice the legendary woman must make. She will not let anything get in the way of her calling from God.

There is a lot of wisdom for the legendary woman contained in Beth Moore's words. Our society does condition us to be victims, but we are called to be overcomers. We are warriors, locked in a battle "against principalities, against powers, against the rulers of the darkness of this age, against spiritual hosts of wickedness in the heavenly places" (Eph. 6:12). We are called to surrender. It's time to stop being offended and start being an offering.

YOUR DEFINING MOMENT

You are more than a conqueror. God has equipped you to fulfill His calling on your life. It's time to shake yourself from the dust. God has already unlocked your shackles, so "loose yourself from the bonds of your neck" (Isa. 52:2). It's time to "be strong in the Lord and in the power of His might" (Eph. 6:10). It's time to put on the armor of God and fight the good fight until you are victorious. So put on the truth of the Word, put on righteousness, put on peace, put on salvation. Take up your shield of faith and the sword of the Spirit (Eph. 6:14–17). Pray with perseverance. Walk in freedom.

Your defining moment as a legendary woman with an overcoming heart will come when you decide that victory is the only option. It will come when you decide that you are going to use every gift that God has given you to passionately pursue your purpose, no matter what the enemy throws against you—his fiery darts don't stand a chance against your fiery faith. Your defining moment will come when you resolutely set your face toward your God-given destiny. Legendary women carry a breakthrough spirit! If there is a wall standing in your way, break through it.

You are a legendary woman who will leave a legacy of the power of God to rescue, redeem, renew, and restore. Your legacy will show there is nothing that is too hard for God. No shame, no shackles, no sin, and no sorry excuses will keep you from your purpose. Other legendary women who look at your life will see what it means to push through and press on. They will see what it means to pursue, overtake, and recover. They will see not only your faith in the goodness of God but also evidence of that abundant goodness in your life.

So keep running. Keep your hand to the plow. Be strong and courageous. In this world you will have trouble, but take heart because Jesus has overcome the world. And God has positioned you to be victorious, for it is your faith that is the victory that overcomes the world.

Prayer for Grace to Overcome

Jesus, because You have overcome the world, give me the grace to overcome. Lord, I choose to press toward the mark You have set for my life. Lord, anoint me with grace to overcome. Jesus, You are the breaker. Anoint me with a breakthrough spirit. I will not break down, but I will break through. I will not give up or give in to the schemes of the enemy, but I will rise up in the power and might of the Lord! I understand it is not by might or power that mountains in my life will be removed but by Your Spirit. I shout grace, grace to weariness. I will be relentless in my pursuit of Your will. I am victorious in You. If I fall, Your grace will pick me up. If I fail, Your mercy will restore me. Father, be my very present help in times of trouble. Let hope arise in my heart. You are the anchor of my soul. I will be steadfast and unmovable, always abounding in Your work. I will not faint, because I believe I will see Your goodness in my life.

Declarations of Victory Over the Enemy

I will not be overcome, but I will overcome.

I will pursue and overtake the enemy, and I will recover all.

I am more than a conqueror.

I will not give up.

All things are possible with God.

I am equipped to go over and exceedingly above in my victory.

I run my race with endurance.

God gives me victory through my Lord Jesus Christ.

God hears me.

My effective, fervent prayer avails much.

I will overcome the temptation to compromise and settle for less than God's best for me.

No matter what obstacles I face, I will fulfill my calling anyway.

The enemy can't stop me. His fiery darts don't stand a chance against my fiery faith.

I know who I am because I know whose I am.

No weapon formed against me shall prosper.

I passionately pursue my purpose.

I carry a breakthrough spirit.

My faith is the victory that overcomes the world.

PART II

Walking in the Fullness of God's Design

Chapter 13

LET THEM HAVE DOMINION

Finding Strength in Unity

So God created man in His own image; in the image
of God He created him; male and female He created
them. Then God blessed them, and God said to them,
"Be fruitful and multiply; fill the earth and subdue it."

—GENESIS 1:27–28

EN AND WOMEN struggle to understand each other
and to thrive together as God intended. I believe
this is a result of the fall of Adam and Eve. God's
design in the Garden of Eden was to have the male and the
female together nurture and steward the earth. Women around
the world often suffer under the assumption they have a lower
status and a less useful purpose than their male counterparts.
Men, on the other hand, often suffer from feeling alone in their
positions of leadership and in the struggles of life's battlefields.
But there is greatness and power on the horizon when we walk
together.

Gender wars are destructive. Nurturing and governing the
earth and our generations according to God's plan requires
a unity of maleness and femaleness to execute God's charge.
While society may continue to battle in this area, it is our
mandate in the body of Christ to operate as one unit, just like
the Trinity. Together They have an intimate connection, and
together They thrive. Men and women in the body of Christ
need to pursue the same unity.

When looking at the roles of men and women, both in marriage and generally, there is a lot of confusion. The concept of

submission is reviled, especially because of past abuses, and our culture promotes rebellion and selfishness over submission in multiple arenas, especially in marriage. And misunderstanding of the biblical roles of men and women has led many, men and women alike, to view women as being of lesser value and worth than men. But God was intentional in His design of men and women and their roles. The Lord values both men and women, and He wants us to have a clear understanding of His design for us.

In the beginning God created man and woman in His image:

> Then God said, "Let Us make man in Our image, according to Our likeness; let them have dominion over the fish of the sea, over the birds of the air, and over the cattle, over all the earth and over every creeping thing that creeps on the earth." So God created man in His own image; in the image of God He created him; male and female He created them. Then God blessed them, and God said to them, "Be fruitful and multiply; fill the earth and subdue it; have dominion over the fish of the sea, over the birds of the air, and over every living thing that moves on the earth."
>
> —GENESIS 1:26–28

On initially reading this passage, one might assume the first sentence means that only men were created in the image of God and given dominion. But as you read further, the passage clearly states that God gave dominion to both males and females, meaning that the use of the word *man* in the first sentence is referring to all humans rather than just males, and the pronoun *them* refers to both men and women. So in the beginning, when God created the heavens and the earth and everything in them, He gave dominion to all humans, both men and women.

Genesis chapter 2 then lays out the basis of the woman's relationship to the man:

> And the LORD God said, "It is not good that man should be alone; I will make him a helper comparable to him."
> —GENESIS 2:18

The word translated "helper" is the Hebrew word *'ēzer*. And it does indeed mean help.[1] Some have interpreted that to mean that women are inferior to men. However, that is not the case. The Hebrew word "refers to one with superior power able to meet a serious need."[2] In fact of the twenty-one times the word is used in the Old Testament, sixteen times are in reference to God. For example, Psalm 70:5 says, "But I am poor and needy; make haste to me, O God! You are my help and my deliverer," and the word for *help* is *'ēzer*.[3] So when Genesis 2:18 uses the word *helper*, it is not placing the woman in an inferior position to the man or saying that she is of less worth or value.

Some of the other confusion surrounding this scripture arose from an incorrect understanding of the King James Version translation:

> And the LORD God said, It is not good that the man should be alone; I will make him an help meet for him.
> —GENESIS 2:18, KJV

Between the use of the word *help* and the phrase *for him*, people often again incorrectly assumed this meant the woman was inferior to the man, as if the man had the leading role while the woman was just a supporting actress. But again, the Hebrew paints a different picture. The last Hebrew word of the verse is *neged*. It means in front, as in the part opposite or a counterpart. It also means corresponding to or parallel.[4] None of the meanings of the Hebrew term support the view that the woman is inferior to the man. Instead the meaning supports the idea that the woman corresponds to the man or is his counterpart, and that is reflected in multiple translations of the verse:

> Now the LORD God said, "It is not good (beneficial) for the man to be alone; I will make him a helper [one who balances him—a counterpart who is] suitable and complementary for him."
>
> —GENESIS 2:18, AMP

> Now the Lord God said, It is not good (sufficient, satisfactory) that the man should be alone; I will make him a helper (suitable, adapted, complementary) for him.
>
> —GENESIS 2:18, AMPC

> Then the LORD God said, "It is not good for the man to be alone. I will make a helper corresponding to him."
>
> —GENESIS 2:18, CSB

> Then the LORD God said, "It is not good for the man to be alone. I will make a helper as his complement."
>
> —GENESIS 2:18, HCSB

> And the LORD God said, "It is not good that man should be alone; I will make him a helper comparable to him."
>
> —GENESIS 2:18

> Then the LORD God said, "It is not good that the man should be alone; I will make him a helper as his partner."
>
> —GENESIS 2:18, NRSV

> And Jehovah God saith, "Not good for the man to be alone, I do make to him an helper—as his counterpart."
>
> —GENESIS 2:18, YLT

So the woman was created as a helper for man, but that does not mean she is inferior. In fact God Himself, in the form of the Holy Spirit, is referred to as the Helper (John 14:16, 26; 15:26; 16:7). And if the Holy Spirit is considered a helper, how could that role ever be considered a lesser one? Can you imagine what life as a believer in Christ would be like without the Holy Spirit? While it may be considered normal for one who helps or assists to be considered weaker or even inferior, the role of helper is a vital one. As Bible teacher Barbara Hughes noted:

> By addressing the Holy Spirit as a helper, Jesus forever elevated the position of the one who assists. Trace the Holy Spirit's actions through the New Testament, and you'll find the Spirit repeatedly encouraging, comforting, coming alongside, and helping. The work of the Holy Spirit, the Helper, is beautiful! And women are never more regal and lovely than when they follow His example, cherishing their responsibility as helper.
>
> So Christian wives [and other Christian women] must never resent or despise the term "helper" or consider it demeaning. To help is divine![5]

In their role as helpers, women are a feminine expression of the nature of God. While God is referred to with masculine pronouns, He has characteristics that are feminine. One of His names is El Shaddai, and while there is disagreement among scholars as to the etymology of the word *shaddai*, one possibility is that it comes from the Hebrew word *šad*, meaning breast, specifically the breast of a nursing mother.[6] In Isaiah 49:15 God's compassion is compared to that of a nursing mother. And in Isaiah 66:13 the Lord says, "As one whom his mother comforts, so I will comfort you." Women are made in the image of God, and while they are different from men, at times reflecting different characteristics of the nature of God, women are not of lesser value than men.

The worth and value of women is clearly seen in the Bible. Jesus clearly demonstrated how much He valued them. He treated them as human beings made in the image of God rather than as second-class citizens, a behavior that was unusual for the time period. For example, a man speaking directly to a woman in public was quite uncommon. In fact when Jesus spoke with the Samaritan woman at the well, "His disciples came, and they marveled that He talked with a woman" (John 4:27). But Jesus not only spoke to the woman at the well; He also spoke to the widow of Nain (Luke 7:13), the woman caught in adultery (John 8:10–11), the woman who had a spirit of infirmity for eighteen years (Luke 13:12), the woman with the issue of blood (Matt. 9:22), and several others recorded in the Gospels. Jesus also demonstrated great love for women in how He spoke to them, addressing them with compassion and care, and desiring to see them set free. Jesus showed women honor and treated them with dignity and respect. Jesus also demonstrated how much He valued women by choosing a woman, Mary Magdalene, to be the first eyewitness of His resurrection (John 20:14–16). The next witnesses were also women (Matt. 28:9; Luke 24:1–10).

In 1 Peter 3:7, Peter described the wife as "the weaker vessel." But he wasn't being derogatory or demeaning to women. The word translated "vessel" is the Greek word *skeuos*.[7] The word is used other places in the Word to refer to both men and women. For example, 2 Corinthians 4:7 says, "We have this treasure in earthen vessels, that the excellence of the power may be of God and not of us." Both men and women are referred to as earthen vessels, meaning they are both capable of being easily broken. And while the Greek word translated "weaker" in 1 Peter 3:7 does indeed mean weak or without strength,[8] it does not mean that men are strong vessels and women are weak vessels. In contrast it means that both men and women are weak vessels. But it also points to the fact that generally men are physically stronger than women. That is just a statement of fact, not a condemnation of women. In fact Peter's reason for pointing out that fact was actually for the benefit of women. The entire verse reads as follows:

> Husbands, likewise, dwell with them with understanding, giving honor to the wife, as to the weaker vessel, and as being heirs together of the grace of life, that your prayers may not be hindered.
>
> —1 Peter 3:7

The word translated "honor" in this verse is *timē*. It means value, valuable, esteem, or precious. It also means "a valuing by which the price is fixed."[9] In other words, the Lord values women, and that value cannot be changed. They are precious. They are valuable. They are esteemed. And the husband is to honor his wife by treating her as valuable and precious. In fact husbands were charged by Peter to not take advantage of the fact that wives are generally physically weaker. And given this was written in a time when women were susceptible to all kinds of abuse from their husbands without any recourse, as they were often viewed as property, Peter was actually elevating the status of women. They weren't property; they were vessels of the Holy Spirit and heirs of grace, just as men were. Peter even pointed out that mistreatment of women would hinder the prayers of men.

Elsewhere in Scripture, something Paul wrote is also used as justification for viewing women as inferior and mistreating them: "Wives, submit to your husbands" (Eph. 5:22). But again, there is more to the passage than just that statement. Ephesians 5:22 through 6:9—which covers wives, husbands, children, parents, servants, and masters—is a detailed explanation of what Paul wrote in Ephesians 5:21: "...submitting to one another in the fear of God." And it is important to note that Paul didn't just give instructions about what submission looks like for wives, children, and servants. He spoke to wives *and* husbands, children *and* parents, servants *and* masters. Even when you are in a leadership position, you should still be submitted to God, and that should have a great effect upon your treatment of those you are leading.

Ephesians 5:21 and 22 use the same word for *submit*. When Paul said that wives should submit to their husbands, it was just one detail in a larger picture. As believers we are called to submit to one another. And the motivation for this submission is fear, or reverence, of the Lord. Submission is an attitude of the heart that recognizes that God is ultimately the One we are submitting to.

And Paul reiterated this in his instructions to wives. He didn't just tell them to submit to their husbands. He wrote, "Wives, submit to your own husbands, *as to the Lord*" (Eph. 5:22, emphasis added). The submission of wives to their husbands also begins to paints a picture of Christ's relationship with the church. But it is Paul's instructions to husbands in the context of submitting to one another that fills in most of the details of Christ's relationship with the church:

> Husbands, love your wives, just as Christ also loved the church and gave Himself for her, that He might sanctify and cleanse her with the washing of water by the word, that He might present her to Himself a glorious church, not having spot or wrinkle or any such thing, but that she should be holy and without blemish. So husbands ought to love their own wives as their own bodies; he who loves his wife loves himself. For no one ever hated his own flesh, but nourishes and cherishes it, just as the Lord does the church. For we are members of His body, of His flesh and of His bones. "For this reason a man shall leave his father and mother and be joined to his wife, and the two shall become one flesh." This is a great mystery, but I speak concerning Christ and the church. Nevertheless let each one of you in particular so love

his own wife as himself, and let the wife see that she respects her husband.

—EPHESIANS 5:25–33

Paul's words make it clear that his intention in instructing wives to submit to their husbands was not that they would be abused, beaten, cut down, destroyed, or mistreated in any other way. Husbands, out of submission to God, are called to love their wives the way they love themselves and to be willing to give themselves up for their wives. They are to nourish and cherish their wives, physically, emotionally, and spiritually. When a husband and wife are submitted to each other and to the Lord, and they are fulfilling their God-given roles, their marriage paints a beautiful picture of Christ's love for the church.

Beyond the immediate context of Paul's instructions to wives there is also the larger context of the entire letter to the Ephesians. Paul told the Ephesians to do the following things, among many others: walk in good works (2:10); "be strengthened with might through His Spirit in the inner man" (3:16); "walk worthy of the calling with which you were called, with all lowliness and gentleness, with longsuffering" (4:1–2); bear with one another in love (4:2); speak the truth in love (4:15); do your share (4:16); be kind, tenderhearted, and forgiving (4:32); "be imitators of God" (5:1); and find out what is acceptable to the Lord (5:10). He also told them not to do the following, again among many other things: continue your corrupt behavior from before you were saved (4:22); lie (4:25); sin in anger or go to bed angry (4:26); steal (4:28); speak corrupt words (4:29); be bitter, wrathful, angry, clamorous, or malicious (4:31); fornicate or be covetous (5:3); have "fellowship with the unfruitful works of darkness" (5:11); or get drunk (5:18).

Once again, when we look at the context of Paul's words in Ephesians 5:22–24, it is clear that wives are to be valued and treated with love and respect by their husbands, just as husbands are to be valued and treated with love and respect by their wives.

The way Christ defends, protects, cherishes, prays for, and goes to war for the church indicates the unmatched value He sees in its thriving and flourishing. Similarly, husbands ought to see that this is the value Christ wants them to have for their wives, defending, protecting, cherishing, praying for, and going to war for them. This also applies by extension to the way men treat women in general.

THE POWER OF ONE

There is great power when a man and a woman have dominion and work together. God's heart for man and woman having dominion is not about one of them dominating the other. It is about the two of them using their individual strengths in unity, because there is great power when the man and woman act as one.

Take for example Abraham and Sarah. They both had great faith, but they had other strengths that were unique. Sarah, for example, had discernment. After Isaac was born, Sarah saw Ishmael scoffing. She recognized that Ishmael's attitude posed a threat to Isaac as Abraham's true heir, the son of promise. So she told Abraham to send Hagar and Ishmael away. This initially displeased Abraham, but God told him that Sarah's discernment was right on the mark. The Lord told Abraham, "Whatever Sarah has said to you, listen to her voice" (Gen. 21:12). One of Abraham's strengths was obeying God. Sarah's discernment and Abraham's obedience, working together, was powerful, ensuring the safety of Isaac's position as Abraham's heir. Their unity made them a power couple.

Another biblical example of a power couple is Priscilla and Aquila. They are always mentioned together in the Bible. They were always shown working together and in unity. They were tentmakers, and they worked together (Acts 18:3–4). A church met in their house, so they hosted the body of believers together. They traveled together at one point with Paul, and apparently they also together risked their lives for Paul (Rom. 16:3). Together they instructed Apollos "[in] the way of God more accurately" (Acts 18:26). Although we don't know for sure, according to tradition they were even martyred together. Everything they did in Scripture, they did together. They were another power couple, using their strengths in unity to benefit the kingdom of God.

Both of these power couples learned how to walk together to fulfill the covenant purposes of God, and the end result was blessing. I believe God is raising up power couples today who will work together, respecting and celebrating each other's strengths, and just as it was with the biblical power couples, the end result will be blessing. They will stand together to receive their promise from God, just as Abraham and Sarah did. They will labor in unity to expand the kingdom, just as Aquila and Priscilla did. They will harness the power of one.

BETTER TOGETHER

God is raising up men and women who can work together as power teams. God is anointing mighty men of valor who will champion and support women in their callings. These men will help liberate women to fulfill their God-given roles in ministries. They understand that God wants a complete picture of His rulership and image revealed in the earth. The church needs both women and men who are willing to passionately pursue their purposes. The church needs mothers *and* fathers, both natural and spiritual, for without them this generation will become dysfunctional.

God did not create women to do everything men can do, nor did God create men to do everything women can do. While men and women are equals, are counterparts, that equality does not mean they are the same. Equality means each person is valued at the same level as another for his or her unique contribution. The very differences we have are our greatest strengths when recognized and used effectively. We are better together, and while there has been improvement in the acknowledgement of that fact, we still have further to go.

The enemy of our souls is the author of separation, division, and strife between men and women. God intended for us to move and work together, but Satan does everything in his power to prevent that from happening, for even Satan recognizes that men and women are better together.

When the feminist movement began, its intent was to empower women and foster needed societal changes for women. But the movement shifted from empowering women to hating men. Any movement without God, no matter how good the original intent, will end up a tool of the enemy. Empowering women to fulfill their God-given purposes is a good thing; teaching women to hate men is not a good thing.

As legendary women, we cannot let any man-hating spirits rule in our lineage. This is vital. Man-hating spirits bring curses on women and families. Hating men causes division, confusion, strife, blame, accusations, and broken families. When Satan first brought division between a man and a woman, it also resulted in the man and woman no longer being in the presence of God.

Our souls were designed to benefit from the nurture of both a mother and a father. God's ideal for the family is for there to be a mother and a father. The division between men and women that results in broken families is not good for our children. With every successive generation more and more children are being raised without fathers, and it is having a profound effect. Children raised without a father are more likely to live in poverty, abuse drugs and alcohol, have physical and emotional health problems, drop out of school, engage in criminal activity, and be sexually active as adolescents.[10] This is not a criticism of single mothers, because heaven knows they have a difficult task. Rather, it is a wake-up call. There are many causes of fatherlessness, with different root issues, but one of the causes is man-hating, and that issue can be dealt with. Breaking the curse of man-hating off your lineage will set you and your children free, with far-reaching effects for your family line.

Having a healthy view of men and their role in your life brings blessing, while man-hating brings curses. Having a healthy view of men fosters unity, respect, responsibility, and peace. It helps families stay together. And most importantly, it pleases God. It is His will for us to move and work together, for we are indeed better together.

The legendary woman must know her own value as a woman, but she also must recognize the value of the men in her life, especially those in a leadership role. Blame shifting and competition must be destroyed so she can leave a legacy of recognizing the value God has placed in both women and men.

Men too have a great responsibility. Men who hold power must take active leadership in discipling, mentoring, encouraging, and advocating for women. They must listen and help. When we come together in unity and mutually respect and depend on each other's unique gifts, we begin to express the complete image of God in the earth, breaking cultural stereotypes and creating a legacy that empowers women to lead with love.

We are insufficient in life without the benefit of both men and women coexisting on equal planes. We are insufficient in communities and in the church without the fully functioning strengths of both men and women. The nature of the female and the nature of the male are each a reflection of something unique and powerful in the character of God. The differences should be celebrated. By dismissing the differences, the distinctive strengths each gender brings to create balanced and healthy homes and church cultures can be lost.

Women were created to express God's rule and reign in the feminine form. Godly femininity is nonthreatening; it doesn't seek to intimidate. Godly femininity is power under control. God has mantled women with the gift of leadership to influence and impact the world for good. God created women to be nurturers. We were designed to influence and inspire those in our spheres with godly wisdom and encouragement. We are helpers. We support and champion the dreams and visions of those we are called to influence. We are legendary women, and we have a legacy to leave.

Legendary women are the ones who will believe God for the restoration of His design for men and women to have dominion in the earth as one. Legendary women will rule and reign in the earth alongside and in partnership with men. We will see their faith, their tenacity, and their love of God demolish the ancient war between men and women in the earth.

Chapter 14

BREAKING THE GLASS
CEILING IN THE CHURCH

The Muzzles Are Coming Off

The Lord gave the word; great was the company of
women who proclaimed it.

—PSALM 68:11, MEV

G OD IS MAKING room for the gifts of women in every
area of life. That includes leading and serving in the
body of Christ. God is shattering every invisible glass
box, ceiling, and barrier to women being key leaders in the
church. The religious misogynistic spirit is one more shrew
to be tamed, one more Goliath that must fall, and one more
behemoth that must be dismantled and destroyed—and it will
be defeated. Women are not just children's church workers or
Sunday school teachers. We are apostles, prophets, evangelists,
teachers, and yes, even pastors.

God is making room in the consciences of men and bringing
revelation to destroy decades of oppressive doctrinal teaching in
one generation. No longer will women be trapped by tradition—
tradition that is not connected to the truth and that requires
women to be quiet, subservient members of the body of Christ.
Legendary women will arise and confront unfair systems and
ideas. They will offer solutions and paradigm-shifting vision that
will cause society to think outside the box of limitations and fear.

But where do those limitations come from? We have already
established that God values women. He has given them unique
gifts and callings for the work of His kingdom. So why have

women been prohibited for so long from being leaders in the church? Why aren't they permitted to teach and preach? Why have they been silenced in the body of Christ? Why do things such as John MacArthur telling Beth Moore to "go home" continue to occur?[1]

There are two passages of Scripture that are the basis of the view that women should keep silent in church and not teach or have authority over men. The first is from the Book of 1 Corinthians:

> Let your women keep silent in the churches, for they are not permitted to speak; but they are to be submissive, as the law also says. And if they want to learn something, let them ask their own husbands at home; for it is shameful for women to speak in church.
>
> —1 CORINTHIANS 14:34–35

Taken at face value and taken out of context, this would seem like a clear prohibition of women speaking in church. And viewed from a broad perspective, the command to keep silent would mean that women couldn't pray out loud, worship, prophesy, teach, preach, or even make an announcement in church. But is that what Paul meant? Does it line up with the rest of Scripture?

Well, earlier in the letter to the Corinthians, Paul wrote about women praying and prophesying when he addressed the issue of head coverings (1 Cor. 11:5). It is clear there that he doesn't have a problem with women praying and prophesying. But both praying and prophesying involve speaking, so Paul couldn't mean that women shouldn't open their mouths in church, as some interpret 1 Corinthians 14 to mean. The immediate context of 1 Corinthians 14:34–35 is order during church meetings, which means Paul was addressing something specific that was interrupting the service. Since Paul was giving instructions to "all the churches of the saints" (v. 33), it was an issue that affected all the churches of the time.

When the church began in the first century, most of the believers were Jewish, so it is not surprising that they had separate seating for men and women, following the pattern of Jewish synagogues. That meant if a woman had a question for her husband in the middle of the sermon, it was not possible to jot him a quick note or discreetly whisper a question in his ear. Viewed in this light, it appears that there was a problem with women being disruptive with the questions, a view supported by the verb tense of the Greek word translated "speak." It is in the present active infinitive, meaning to continually speak.[2]

Although it is a good thing for both women and men to be engaged with the teaching of the Word and to have questions about it, it is not good for those questions to interrupt the learning of others. Paul's prohibition was meant to keep order by preventing women from shouting questions to their husbands during the teaching. Instead, when they had questions—which likely happened often since in Judaism at the time women did not have regular and open access to the teaching of Scripture—they needed to wait and ask their husbands later at home.

So Paul's instructions were about maintaining order in the church rather than prohibiting women from speaking. Both men and women have spiritual gifts—including the gift of prophecy, which Paul addressed in the verses just before—and the exercise of those gifts should be welcome in the church as long as things are "done decently and in order" (1 Cor. 14:40).

That brings us to the next passage about women and their involvement in the church. While there are many churches that do not have a problem with women praying, prophesying, speaking in tongues, and so on in the church, they draw a line at women teaching and/or having authority over men, based on 1 Timothy 2:12: "And I do not permit a woman to teach or to have authority over a man, but to be in silence."

Again, this seems to be a clear prohibition, but let's take a deeper look. We have already addressed the part about being silent, but what about the rest? How can we interpret it in light of the rest of Scripture?

If we take the first part of the verse, "I do not permit a woman to teach," as a stand-alone command, it doesn't make sense in light of other scriptures. Men and women alike are admonished throughout the Old Testament to teach their children. In his letter to Titus, Paul told the older women to teach the younger women. And the Great Commission (Matt. 28:19–20), given by Jesus to all His disciples, men and women alike, includes "teaching," the same word used in 1 Timothy 2:12.[3]

So Paul didn't mean teaching in general. So did he mean that women can't teach men? While assuming that is true opens up a whole other series of questions (e.g., Does *men* mean all males or males over a certain age? And if it means males over a certain age, what age is that?), if we look at Scripture as a whole, we find examples of women teaching men that are presented in a positive light. For example, in Acts 18, both Priscilla and Aquila instructed Apollos in the way of God, and as a result, Apollos was enabled to "vigorously [refute] the Jews publicly, showing from the Scriptures that Jesus is the Christ" (Acts 18:28). The result of Apollos' instruction from Priscilla and Aquila seems to indicate that they did not just have a casual conversation; rather, Apollos was taught "the way of God more accurately" with depth and clarity (v. 26).

I believe the key to understanding what Paul was saying in 1 Timothy 2:12 lies in the word translated "have authority." The word is *authenteō*, and it means to "usurp authority."[4] Usurp means "to seize and hold...by force or without right; to take the place of by or as if by force."[5] If we look at the beginning of Paul's letter to Timothy, we see that Timothy was told to "charge some that they teach no other doctrine" (1 Tim. 1:3). I believe 1 Timothy 2:12 is a further explanation of this. There were women who were teaching false doctrine, and in doing so, they were usurping the authority of those called by God and placed in the church to teach sound doctrine. Godly teachers who know the Lord and know the Word, are full of wisdom, and teach the whole counsel of God with clarity and authority "for doctrine, for reproof, for correction, for instruction in righteousness" are vital to the health and growth of the church, that we "may be complete, thoroughly equipped for every good work" (2 Tim. 3:16–17). Anyone inserting herself (or himself) in the way of sound teaching should be silenced.

Another possible meaning of the word *authenteō* is to originate or be the author of.[6] The adjective form of the word is *authentikos*, from which we get the English word *authentic*.[7] Think about the word *authentic* in terms of something being original. If we take that concept and apply it to the women being addressed in 1 Timothy 2:12, it lines up with a false teaching of Gnosticism, which was a problem in the early church. Among other things, Gnostics believed that Eve was superior to Adam because she "gave [him] life" by calling him out of his deep sleep.[8] In other words, Gnostics believed that the woman was the originator of man. If we plug that meaning into 1 Timothy 2:12, it becomes, "I do not permit a woman to teach or represent herself as originator of man."[9]

Regardless of which meaning of *authenteō* is used, Paul was addressing a specific issue rather than issuing an across-the-board prohibition of women teaching in the church.

It is time to put a stop the misogynistic, patriarchal traditions of men that have hindered women's progress and equality in the body of Christ. It is time to stop labeling godly women as Jezebels or witches because God has given them a gift and a calling to teach or to lead. As Lee Grady noted in *10 Lies the Church Tells Women*:

> It is offensive to suggest that a woman who loves Jesus Christ, walks in personal holiness, and upholds the

Word of God with integrity is influenced by a "spirit of Jezebel"—just because she is female! Yet I have lost count of the number of women who have told me that they were accused of being a "Jezebel influence" because they functioned as a pastor, an evangelist, or even a lay leader.[10]

To be clear, there was a female teacher referred to as Jezebel in the Book of Revelation (2:20). However, she was a false teacher who taught sexual immorality and idolatry. The mere fact that the teacher was a woman did not make her a Jezebel. She was referred to as Jezebel because she was teaching idolatrous, immoral doctrine, just like the Old Testament queen. A woman who rightly divides the Word of truth in pursuit of a God-given calling to teach the Word should not ever be labeled Jezebel merely because she is a woman.

In his letter to the Galatians the apostle Paul wrote that "there is neither Jew nor Greek, there is neither slave nor free, there is neither male nor female; for you are all one in Christ Jesus" (3:28). It is time for the divisions in the church based on gender to end. The body of Christ is diverse, with men and women with a wide variety of gifts, talents, and callings. It is time to celebrate that diversity by being unified in encouraging every believer to wholeheartedly pursue his or her calling and by not being obstacles or barriers to that pursuit.

> For as the body is one and has many members, but all the members of that one body, being many, are one body, so also is Christ. For by one Spirit we were all baptized into one body.
>
> —1 Corinthians 12:12–13

The body of Christ needs to heed the apostle Paul's call to walk in unity.

> I, therefore, the prisoner of the Lord, beseech you to walk worthy of the calling with which you were called, with all

lowliness and gentleness, with longsuffering, bearing with one another in love, endeavoring to keep the unity of the Spirit in the bond of peace. There is one body and one Spirit, just as you were called in one hope of your calling; one Lord, one faith, one baptism; one God and Father of all, who is above all, and through all, and in you all.

—Ephesians 4:1–6

Therefore if there is any consolation in Christ, if any comfort of love, if any fellowship of the Spirit, if any affection and mercy, fulfill my joy by being like-minded, having the same love, being of one accord, of one mind. Let nothing be done through selfish ambition or conceit, but in lowliness of mind let each esteem others better than himself. Let each of you look out not only for his own interests, but also for the interests of others.

—Philippians 2:1–4

It is time for men in the body of Christ, especially those in leadership, to recognize the gifts and callings of their sisters in Christ. It is time for men to offer encouragement rather than discouragement and support rather than criticism.

When people in the church think of a biblical example of the ideal woman, they often think of the woman described in Proverbs 31, commonly referred to as the virtuous woman. The word translated "virtuous" in Proverbs 31:10 is *chayil*. It occurs 243 times in the Old Testament and is translated in the sense of virtuous only four times, all in reference to women (Ruth 3:11; Prov. 12:4; 31:10, 29). The overwhelming majority of the time it means army, man of valor, strength, power, valiant, mighty.[11]

While I am sure most men would not be threatened by a virtuous woman, I believe there are quite a few in the church who would be threatened by a valiant, strong, powerful, mighty woman. But it is time for that attitude to change. It is time for men in the church to put the other meanings of *chayil* into

191

Proverbs 31:10 and still view the woman described as worth far more than rubies. A valiant woman has worth far above rubies. A strong woman has worth far above rubies. A powerful woman has worth far above rubies. A mighty woman has worth far above rubies. Rather than being threatened by strong, legendary women, men in the church need to esteem them.[12]

The church has a long tradition of viewing women as inferior to men and as incapable of teaching or preaching the Word. Men have allowed that traditional view to affect their actions, even to the point of translating the Word of God to fit that view. When the translators of the King James Bible translated Psalm 68:11, the verse read, "The Lord gave the word; great was the company of those that published it." However, the Hebrew word translated "those who published it" is a feminine plural.[13] In other words, the Hebrew clearly refers to "women" rather than the neutral "those." It's as if the men couldn't imagine women not only being given the word but also publishing or proclaiming it. And because Bible translations often follow the tradition of the King James Version, of the fifty-four English versions of the Bible on Bible Gateway, only thirty-two mention women in that verse.[14]

This is not meant to disparage the King James Version or any other translation. It is meant to draw attention to the fact that it's past time to put an end to church traditions that place women in a position of inferiority and incapability. Each member of the body of Christ needs to esteem the other members and not attribute lesser value to them based on gender. God has put legendary women with gifts that include teaching and preaching in the church for the furtherance of His kingdom. The church needs to let them use their gifts the way God directs them to, not the way traditions dictate.

For the Lord has given the word, and great will be the company of legendary women who proclaim it (Ps. 68:11, MEV).

Chapter 15

LEAVING A LEGACY

Your Story Matters

A good man [or woman] leaves an inheritance to his
children's children.

—PROVERBS 13:22

G OD IS AWAKENING an army of legendary women who
will become mothers of the nation. This generation needs spiritual mothers who conceive and bring
forth the plans and purposes of God the way Sarah—wife of
Abraham and mother of Isaac—did. There has been broad
acceptance of the need for spiritual fathers, but if we are to
see the order of God established in the earth, it's going to take
apostolic mothering grace as well.

Legendary women who carry an anointing like Sarah's will
have a passion to create a natural and spiritual legacy. Sarah
was a woman chosen by God to give birth to a new nation.
She had unshakable faith in an unshakable God. She believed
that through her all the families of the earth would be blessed.
Sarah was a courageous pioneer who went on the adventure of
a lifetime. Sarah was a legendary woman who left a legacy of
faith, love, and honor for male authority.

What type of legacy will you leave for the generations to
follow? *Merriam-Webster* defines *legacy* as "something trans-
mitted by or received from an ancestor or predecessor or from
the past." It is also defined as a bequest, or a gift.[1] Your legacy
is the enduring gift you pass on to the generations that will
come after you. Legendary women focus on leaving a legacy

that will endure. They pass on things of lasting, eternal value. Legacy involves living intentionally and aiming to build into and build up the next generations for their success.

When you realize the power and value of your spiritual legacy, God begins to birth in you an awareness that your actions matter. Your character matters. Your faith matters. Your life matters. *You* matter. Legacy is not about material possessions—legendary women live by a different value system. Legendary women are women of value who add value to others. But again, you must be intentional about the legacy you want to leave behind. You must live by the conviction that one woman can and will make a difference in the earth.

Have you ever thought about what your great-grandchildren will say about you thirty years after Jesus has called you home, what legacy you are leaving your family, your community, your culture, or the world? I believe God is releasing a great awakening in women to define, decide, and craft their legacies. Legendary women will live and establish kingdom principles that can be passed on to future generations of women.

The legendary women of today need to claim their inheritance from the legendary women of the past. Like the daughters of Zelophehad, they need to step forward and say in boldness, "The legacy of courage, love, faith, obedience, wisdom, generosity, destiny, and victory belongs to us. We are the daughters of the legendary women of the past, so we claim their legacy as our God-given inheritance." By claiming their inheritance, legendary women are able to leave an inheritance to future generations of legendary women.

Legendary women are on a godly quest on behalf of future generations. Their example is vital. Seeing legendary women who have godly character and exercise their God-given gifts is good not only for our daughters but also for our sons. It benefits the entire body of Christ to see the full expression of God through the lives and fully realized dreams and aspirations of women. And when legendary women use their exceptional character and giftings to pursue the callings of God on their lives, it ensures they will pass on an amazing spiritual inheritance.

Part of the mandate of the legendary woman is to protect and defend the next generation with her courage and passion for justice, to guide them with her wisdom and discernment, to comfort and heal them with her love and compassion, to teach them with her obedience, and to inspire them with her faith and her victory.

We all love a good story. Books like *Chicken Soup for the Soul* have become best sellers because of the way the stories inspire us, make us think, touch our hearts, and so on. And not only do we all love a story, but we all have a story. Your place as a legendary woman is tied to your story. Your story is important. Whether your story is spectacular and full of gut-wrenching drama or simple, your story matters whether you think so or not.

You may think your story isn't important because you weren't a victim of human trafficking or homeless or kidnapped by terrorists or rescued from a near-fatal accident of newsworthy proportions. But your story matters. It matters because you matter. It matters because no matter what your life looked like before Jesus, your life looks different now.

Everyone comes to Jesus with baggage and burdens, pain and problems. But Jesus set you free—from sin, from judgment, from bondage, from despair. He gave you grace and mercy you did not deserve. He loved you exactly how you were, but He also loved you too much to leave you that way. He chose you. He accepted you. He freed you. He called you. He filled you with His Spirit. And that is a great story!

When the Israelites crossed over the Jordan into the Promised Land, they took twelve stones from the midst of the river to set up as a reminder of the great things God had done. They were memorial stones. When their children asked their parents why the stones were there, the parents had an opportu- nity to tell their children of the goodness of God (Josh. 4:1–7).

Legendary woman, you are a memorial stone. You are a reminder of the great things God has done. When your chil- dren ask you questions about your story and how you came to be where you are, both physically and spiritually, you have an opportunity to tell them of the goodness and faithfulness of God. Your story is your legacy. It doesn't have to be newsworthy in the eyes of the world. In fact the stories of most legendary women are not newsworthy in the eyes of the world. They were just regular women who said yes to God. They were faithful. They executed small things that in the eyes of heaven were big things. Their love and obedience pleased their Father in heaven.

Legendary women are not heroes who happen to be female or who defiantly renounce their female identity to bravely enter the male domain in pursuit of success and power. Rather, their feminine identity is an essential factor in their contributions to the course of history. There is a saying in the Talmud that who- ever saves a life saves the whole world. That would also mean that if you change one life, you change the world. Legendary women are faithful to be exactly who God made them to be, and they change the world one person at a time. They have a positive and constructive impact simply by being willing ves- sels for the Lord.

While we have come far in enabling women to fulfill their God-given callings, we have further to go. The enemy has used fear, intimidation, and feelings of insecurity, inadequacy, and inferiority to keep women from their divine purposes for far too long. It is time for you and me and all the other legendary women in the body of Christ to proclaim that "God has not given us a spirit of fear, but of power and of love and of a sound mind" (2 Tim. 1:7).

It is time for legendary women to rise up and overcome the accuser. Revelation tells us that "they overcame [the accuser] by the blood of the Lamb and by the word of their testimony" (12:11). And that is how you, legendary woman, will overcome. It is how you will gain the victory. The blood of Jesus, the Lamb of God slain for the sins of the world, and the word of your testimony will overcome anything Satan tries to throw against you. It will overcome doubt. It will overcome despair. It will overcome defeat.

And just in case you still think your story doesn't really matter, realize that *testimony* is another word for the story of what Jesus has done for, in, and with you. It is your eyewitness record of the grace and mercy of God at work in your life. It is your personal record of the abundance of His love. It is evidence of His unfathomable goodness and unmatched faithfulness. And your story is powerful enough that when it is combined with the blood of Jesus, victory over the enemy is guaranteed.

So tell your story, legendary woman. Inspire the next generation of legendary women. Leave a legacy. Be a *chayil* woman, both virtuous and strong. Be a woman of character and gifting working together. Be courageous. Be a woman of fierce love and driving compassion. Be a woman of fiery faith. Be obedient. Be confrontational. Be discerning and wise. Be a master negotiator. Be an extravagant giver. Be a silent soldier. Be poured out. Be destiny driven. Be a woman with an overcomer's heart. Be legendary.

YOUR MOMENT HAS COME

LEGENDARY WOMAN, YOUR moment has come. God has brought you to this moment on purpose. Everything in your life has been working together for your good because you have been called according to His purpose.

You live in a culture in which everyone wants to brand you and fit you in a box. Society may put all kinds of labels on you, but those labels don't matter. What matters is what God says about you. You are His daughter. You are precious in His sight. You are of more value than rubies. You are fearfully and wonderfully made. You are *chayil*—virtuous, valiant, and strong. You are special. You are chosen. You are a woman of God.

And you were made to be a legendary woman. So let the Holy Spirit develop and define the attributes of the legendary woman in you. Let Him help you to let your character and your gifting shine through your life in equal measure. It's time to take your rightful place in a culture that is sometimes hostile and unwelcoming to women. God is unlocking your personal gifts, talents, and power. God is building in you the capacity to walk in your God-given mandate to subdue the earth and have dominion. He is breaking the insecurity and confusion regarding your measure of rule in the earth.

You may feel invisible or unvalued in a culture that judges you based on worldly standards. You may feel as if the things you do have little to no effect on the world around you. But the truth is that God sees you. He formed you when you were in your mother's womb (Ps. 139:13). He has redeemed you because of the value He places on you, and He calls you by name (Isa. 43:1). Even though the world around you may often fail to notice your acts of kindness and mercy and the people you touch with the love of God, the Lord of heaven never fails to notice. He sees it all. He is the God who sees (Gen. 16:13). His thoughts for you outnumber the grains of sand on the shore (Ps. 139:17–18).

Your greatness may be hidden by a shroud of mystery, a scandalous past, or a screen of normalcy as you aspire to live out your destiny and purpose every day. But woman of God, you are greater than you give yourself credit for. With the exception of Pharaoh's daughter, who was born into a palace, the women we looked at throughout this book all started out as just normal women. They had families, jobs, homes, and their own share of challenges. They were wives and widows, mothers and daughters, sisters and friends. They were servants, slaves, tentmakers, nurses, prostitutes, and students. They lived in tents, shacks, and houses, and some were homeless at times. One was blind, one had a seizure disorder, and another is an amputee. None of these things made them legendary. The thing that made them legendary was their willingness to say yes to God.

Historically, women have overcome extraordinary challenges and taken great risks to birth and nurture some of the most amazing people, ventures, causes, and ideas the world has ever known. The Bible is full of examples of world-changing women who took risks to bring about reformation and change. And again, they were normal women. But they were willing vessels. They took a step of faith and said, "Here I am, Lord! Send me!" These women provided a road map of courage, perseverance, and loving their lives even unto death for the purposes of God.

And God is giving flight to the legendary nature within you! A legend is one who inspires. I believe the Lord is raising up women who will accomplish extraordinary things to inspire others to greatness. It will be their legacy.

There are dreams the Spirit of God is challenging you to dream. It is time to embrace your path as a real-life legend, for well-behaved women—in the traditional sense of maintaining an inferior, subservient position in relation to men—seldom make history. You are the expression of God in feminine form. God is causing the beauty and power of women to be on display! You were created in the image of God. Even if you have a dark past or are the unlikeliest of heroes, God will take your story and use it for His glory. Your story matters!

It is time to stop waiting and looking for the life you deserve and start taking the reins. I have found the Christian life is proactive. You must have ascending levels of determination to keep asking the hard questions, seeking solutions, and knocking on the doors of opportunity until they fling wide open for you! The only things that can stop the legendary nature in you from taking flight are internal barriers created by the enemy of your destiny. God is delivering you from insecurity, inferiority, inadequacy, and impostor syndrome (the belief that you have only succeeded by chance rather than because of your gifts and talents). God is anointing you to conquer these inner enemies. You will embrace your purpose and overcome every obstacle that comes to stop the legendary woman inside of you from coming alive.

God is awakening many women today to a purpose greater than themselves. He is calling us from a mundane existence to a place of significance and fulfillment. He is calling us to purpose, to destiny. Many women in the body of Christ have been trapped by tradition or locked into captivity by cultural and gender prejudice. But Jesus came to set you free, and when the Son sets you free, you are free indeed! It is time to shake yourself from the dust, shake off your shackles, and walk out of the prison of tradition into a purpose-filled, destiny-driven, abundant life in Christ.

We have looked at many different defining moments throughout this book. We have considered how to identify your defining moments, as well as how to prepare for your defining moments. But ultimately you will have one key defining moment as a legendary woman. It likely will occur without a spotlight or fanfare. There won't be a parade. People won't see a story about it on the nightly news or read an article about it online. With perhaps a few exceptions, no one on earth will even notice.

But heaven will be a different story. There will be rejoicing in heaven when you have your defining moment, and it will put a smile on the Father's face, for your ultimate defining moment will be when you say yes to God, when you purpose in your heart to overcome any obstacle in your path as you pursue your God-given calling. That is the moment you will become a legendary woman. Will you embrace the call?

NOTES

Introduction

1. *Merriam-Webster*, s.v. "legend," accessed April 19, 2021, https://www.merriam-webster.com/dictionary/legend.
2. Louis Ginzberg, *Legends of the Bible* (Philadelphia: Jewish Publication Society of America, 1956), xi, https://archive.org/details/legendsofbible00ginz/page/n13/mode/2up.
3. Blue Letter Bible, s.v. *"hagios,"* accessed April 14, 2021, https://www.blueletterbible.org/lang/lexicon/lexicon.cfm?page=3&strongs=G40&t=KJV#lexResults.
4. *Merriam-Webster*, s.v. "defining moment," accessed April 19, 2021, https://www.merriam-webster.com/dictionary/defining%20moment.

Chapter 1

1. Blue Letter Bible, s.v. *"pistis,"* accessed April 19, 2021, https://www.blueletterbible.org/lang/lexicon/lexicon.cfm?Strongs=G4102&t=KJV.
2. Blue Letter Bible, s.v. *"prosagōgē,"* accessed April 19, 2021, https://www.blueletterbible.org/lang/lexicon/lexicon.cfm?Strongs=G4318&t=KJV.
3. Joyce Smith with Ginger Kolbaba, *The Impossible: The Miraculous Story of a Mother's Faith and Her Child's Resurrection* (New York: Hachette Book Group, 2017), 242, https://www.amazon.com/Impossible-Miraculous-Mothers-Childs-Resurrection/dp/1478976950.
4. Smith with Kolbaba, *The Impossible*, 33.
5. Smith with Kolbaba, *The Impossible*, 242.
6. Elisabeth Elliot, *These Strange Ashes* (New York: Harper & Row, 1975), 110, https://archive.org/details/thesestrangeashe00elli/page/110/mode/2up?.

Chapter 2

1. *Merriam-Webster*, s.v. "courage," accessed April 19, 2021, https://www.merriam-webster.com/dictionary/courage.

2. Blue Letter Bible, s.v. "*ʾāmēṣ*," accessed April 19, 2021, https://www.blueletterbible.org/lang/Lexicon/Lexicon.cfm?strongs=H553&t=KJV.

3. Matthew 1:1–16 contains the genealogy of Jesus through David's son Solomon. Three kings of Judah were omitted from the genealogy in Matthew. While there are various interpretations of why the three kings, Joash among them, were omitted here, for our purposes here it is enough that Joram was the father of Ahaziah, who was the father of Joash, who was the father of Amaziah, who was the father of Uzziah, also known as Azariah (1 Chron. 3:11–12; Matt. 1:8).

4. Blue Letter Bible, s.v. "*Yᵊhôyāḏāʿ*," accessed April 19, 2021, https://www.blueletterbible.org/lang/lexicon/lexicon.cfm?Strongs=H3077&t=KJV.

5. Blue Letter Bible, s.v. "*Yᵊhôšebaʿ*," accessed April 19, 2021, https://www.blueletterbible.org/lang/lexicon/lexicon.cfm?strongs=H3089&t=KJV.

6. Blue Letter Bible, s.v. "*šābaʿ*," accessed April 19, 2021, https://www.blueletterbible.org/lang/lexicon/lexicon.cfm?strongs=H7650&t=KJV.

7. Bethany Hamilton, "Courage Fueled by Preparation," Soul Surfer & Co, September 8, 2020, https://bethanyhamilton.com/courage-fueled-by-preparation/.

8. Rosa Parks, *Quiet Strength: The Faith, the Hope, and the Heart of a Woman Who Changed a Nation* (Grand Rapids, MI: Zondervan, 1994), 16–17, https://archive.org/details/quietstrengthfai00park/page/16/mode/2up.

9. Parks, *Quiet Strength*, 17–18.

CHAPTER 3

1. *Merriam-Webster*, s.v. "love," accessed April 19, 2021, https://www.merriam-webster.com/dictionary/love.

2. *Merriam-Webster*, s.v. "compassion," accessed April 19, 2021, https://www.merriam-webster.com/dictionary/compassion.

3. Blue Letter Bible, s.v. *"splagchnizomai,"* accessed April 19, 2021, https://www.blueletterbible.org/lang/lexicon/lexicon.cfm?Strongs=G4697&t=KJV.

4. William Davidson Talmud: Sanhedrin 37a, Sefaria, accessed April 19, 2021, https://www.sefaria.org/Sanhedrin.37a?lang=bi.

5. Blue Letter Bible, s.v. *"ḥāmal,"* accessed April 19, 2021, https://www.blueletterbible.org/lang/lexicon/lexicon.cfm?Strongs=H2550&t=KJV.

6. "Mother Teresa," Biography, updated February 24, 2020, https://www.biography.com/religious-figure/mother-teresa.

7. Navin Chawla, *Mother Teresa: The Authorized Biography* (Rockport, MA: Element, 1992), 201, https://archive.org/details/motherteresa00chaw/page/200/mode/2up?q=love.

8. Chawla, *Mother Teresa*, 19.

9. "Meet Rachel," Rachel's Challenge, accessed April 19, 2021, https://rachelschallenge.org/about-us/meet-rachel.

10. Lisa Anderson and Julie Deardorff, "Heart-Wrenching Farewells Begin in Grieving Town," *Chicago Tribune*, April 25, 1999, https://www.chicagotribune.com/news/ct-xpm-1999-04-25-9904250384-story.html.

11. Darrell Scott with Steve Rabey, *Rachel Smiles: The Spiritual Legacy of Columbine Martyr Rachel Scott* (Nashville: Thomas Nelson, 2002), 15, https://archive.org/details/rachelsmilesspir00scot_0/page/14/mode/2up.

12. "About Rachel's Challenge," Rachel's Challenge, accessed April 19, 2021, https://rachelschallenge.org/about-us.

13. Scott with Rabey, *Rachel Smiles*, 157.

14. Blue Letter Bible, s.v. *"Mōše,"* accessed April 19, 2021, https://www.blueletterbible.org/lang/lexicon/lexicon.cfm?Strongs=H4872&t=KJV.

15. Jane George, "Polar Bear No Match for Fearsome Mother in Ivujivik," Nunatsiaq News, February 17, 2006, https://web.archive.org/web/20070927011557/http://www.nunatsiaq.com/archives/60217/news/nunavut/60217_03.html; Alyssa Newcomb, "Super Strength: Daughter

Rescues Dad Pinned Under Car," ABC News, August 1, 2012, https://abcnews.go.com/US/superhero-woman-lifts-car-off-dad/story?id=16907591#.UMay9Hfeba4.

16. Blue Letter Bible, s.v. *"erōtaō,"* accessed April 19, 2021, https://www.blueletterbible.org/lang/lexicon/lexicon.cfm?Strongs=G2065&t=KJV.

17. Martha Vicinus and Bea Nergaard, eds., *Ever Yours, Florence Nightingale* (Cambridge, MA: Harvard University Press, 1990), 49–50, https://archive.org/details/everyoursflorenc0000nigh/page/50/mode/2up.

CHAPTER 4

1. As quoted in Mary Fairchild, "Why Is Obedience to God Important?" Learn Religions, March 17, 2020, https://www.learnreligions.com/obedience-to-god-701962; Rick W. Byargeon, "Obedience," in *Eerdmans Dictionary of the Bible*, ed. David Noel Freedman (Grand Rapids, MI: Wm. B. Eerdmans Publishing Co., 2000).

2. "Sun Minghua," Voice of the Martyrs, accessed April 19, 2021, https://www.prisoneralert.com/pprofiles/vp_prisoner_148_profile.html.

3. "Testimony of Sister Sun Minghua in Jail," China Aid Association, April 12, 2006, https://www.chinaaid.org/2006/04/testimony-of-sister-sun-minghua-in-jail.html.

4. "Asia Bibi," Voice of the Martyrs, accessed April 19, 2021, https://www.prisoneralert.com/pprofiles/vp_prisoner_197_profile.html.

CHAPTER 5

1. *Merriam-Webster*, s.v. "confront," accessed April 19, 2021, https://www.merriam-webster.com/dictionary/confront.

2. *Merriam-Webster* (thesaurus), s.v. "confront," accessed April 19, 2021, https://www.merriam-webster.com/thesaurus/confront.

3. Blue Letter Bible, s.v. *"Maḥlâ,"* accessed April 19, 2021, https://www.blueletterbible.org/lang/lexicon/lexicon.

cfm?Strongs=H4244&t=KJV; Blue Letter Bible, s.v. *"ḥālâ,"* accessed April 19, 2021, https://www.blueletterbible.org/lang/lexicon/lexicon.cfm?strongs=H2470&t=KJV.

4. Blue Letter Bible, s.v. *"Nōʿâ,"* accessed April 19, 2021, https://www.blueletterbible.org/lang/lexicon/lexicon.cfm?Strongs=H5270&t=KJV; Blue Letter Bible, s.v. *"nûaʿ,"* accessed April 19, 2021, https://www.blueletterbible.org/lang/lexicon/lexicon.cfm?strongs=H5128&t=KJV.

5. Blue Letter Bible, s.v. *"Milkâ,"* accessed April 19, 2021, https://www.blueletterbible.org/lang/lexicon/lexicon.cfm?Strongs=H4435&t=KJV.

6. Blue Letter Bible, s.v. *"Tirṣâ,"* accessed April 19, 2021, https://www.blueletterbible.org/lang/lexicon/lexicon.cfm?Strongs=H8656&t=KJV; Blue Letter Bible, s.v. *"rāṣâ,"* accessed April 19, 2021, https://www.blueletterbible.org/lang/lexicon/lexicon.cfm?strongs=H7521&t=KJV.

7. Alexander Cruden, *Cruden's Complete Concordance to the Old and New Testaments* (Grand Rapids, MI: Zondervan, 1953), 795, https://www.google.com/books/edition/Cruden_s_Complete_Concordance_to_the_Old/w4kw0xJZWxEC?hl=en&gbpv=0&bsq.

8. Sojourner Truth, *The Narrative of Sojourner Truth*, ed. Olive Gilbert (Boston: The Author, 1850), https://digital.library.upenn.edu/women/truth/1850/1850.html.

9. Truth, *The Narrative of Sojourner Truth*.

10. Truth, *The Narrative of Sojourner Truth*.

CHAPTER 6

1. *Merriam-Webster*, s.v. "negotiate," accessed April 19, 2021, https://www.merriam-webster.com/dictionary/negotiate.

2. *Merriam-Webster*, s.v. "manipulate," accessed April 19, 2021, https://www.merriam-webster.com/dictionary/manipulate.

3. "Negotiation Advice for Women," Lean In, accessed April 19, 2021, https://leanin.org/negotiation.

4. Blue Letter Bible, s.v. "*šēkel*," accessed April 19, 2021, https://www.blueletterbible.org/lang/lexicon/lexicon. cfm?Strongs=H7922&t=KJV.

5. Blue Letter Bible, s.v. "*Nābāl*," accessed April 19, 2021, https://www.blueletterbible.org/lang/lexicon/lexicon. cfm?Strongs=H5037&t=KJV.

6. Folorunso Alakija, "Woman Thou Art Loosed Conference 2018, Dallas," YouTube video, 58:09, December 27, 2018, https://www.youtube.com/watch?v=Zw1GxjtsrDM.

7. Alakija, "Woman Thou Art Loosed Conference 2018, Dallas."

8. Folorunso Alakija, "Bishop T. D. Jakes interview with Mrs Folorunso Alakija," YouTube video, 24:06, October 24, 2018, https://www.youtube.com/watch?v=Pebjv6Zsi8I.

9. Alakija, "Bishop T. D. Jakes interview with Mrs Folorunso Alakija."

Chapter 7

1. Ronald E. Riggio, "Women's Intuition: Myth or Reality?," *Psychology Today*, July 14, 2011, https://www.psychologytoday.com/us/blog/cutting-edge-leadership/201107/women-s-intuition-myth-or-reality.

2. Blue Letter Bible, s.v. "*bānâ*," accessed April 19, 2021, https://www.blueletterbible.org/lang/lexicon/lexicon. cfm?Strongs=H1129&t=KJV.

3. Blue Letter Bible, s.v. "*bayit*," accessed April 19, 2021, https://www.blueletterbible.org/lang/lexicon/lexicon. cfm?Strongs=H1004&t=KJV.

4. Blue Letter Bible, s.v. "*hāras*," accessed April 19, 2021, https://www.blueletterbible.org/lang/lexicon/lexicon. cfm?Strongs=H2040&t=KJV.

5. *Merriam-Webster*, s.v. "discernment," accessed April 19, 2021, https://www.merriam-webster.com/dictionary/discernment.

6. *Merriam-Webster*, s.v. "discern," accessed April 19, 2021, https://www.merriam-webster.com/dictionary/discern.

7. Blue Letter Bible, s.v. *"aisthēsis,"* accessed April 19, 2021, https://www.blueletterbible.org/lang/lexicon/lexicon. cfm?Strongs=G144&t=KJV.

8. Blue Letter Bible, s.v. *"Rāḥāb,"* accessed April 19, 2021, https://www.blueletterbible.org/lang/lexicon/lexicon. cfm?Strongs=H7343&t=KJV; Blue Letter Bible, s.v. *"rāḥāb,"* accessed April 19, 2021, https://www.blueletterbible.org/lang/lexicon/lexicon.cfm?strongs=H7342&t=KJV.

9. Corrie ten Boom, *The Hiding Place* (Uhrichsville, OH: Barbour and Company, 1971), 21, https://archive.org/details/hidingplac00tenb/mode/2up.

10. Ten Boom, *The Hiding Place*, 211.

11. Ten Boom, *The Hiding Place* (Grand Rapids, MI: Chosen, 2006), 8, https://www.amazon.com/Hiding-Place-Corrie-Ten-Boom/dp/0800794052/ref=sr_1_1?keywords=the+hiding+place&qid=1612972251&sr=8-1.

12. Corrie ten Boom, "Guideposts Classics: Corrie ten Boom on Forgiveness," *Guideposts*, July 24, 2014, https://www.guideposts.org/better-living/positive-living/guideposts-classics-corrie-ten-boom-on-forgiveness.

13. Corrie ten Boom, *Tramp for the Lord* (Fort Washington, PA: Christian Literature Crusade, 1974), 12, https://archive.org/details/trampforlord00tenb/page/12/mode/2up.

CHAPTER 8

1. Blue Letter Bible, s.v. *"penēs,"* accessed April 19, 2021, https://www.blueletterbible.org/lang/lexicon/lexicon. cfm?strongs=G3993&t=KJV.

2. Blue Letter Bible, s.v. *"diakoneō,"* accessed April 19, 2021, https://www.blueletterbible.org/lang/lexicon/lexicon. cfm?Strongs=G1247&t=KJV.

3. Blue Letter Bible, s.v. *"diakoneō."*

4. Blue Letter Bible, s.v. *"sousanna,"* accessed April 19, 2021, https://www.blueletterbible.org/lang/lexicon/lexicon. cfm?Strongs=G4677&t=KJV.

5. Blue Letter Bible, s.v. *"šûšan,"* accessed April 19, 2021, https://www.blueletterbible.org/lang/lexicon/lexicon. cfm?strongs=H7799&t=KJV; Blue Letter Bible, s.v. *"šûš,"* accessed April 19, 2021, https://www.blueletterbible.org/lang/lexicon/lexicon.cfm?strongs=H7797&t=KJV.

6. Blue Letter Bible, s.v. *"iōan(n)a,"* accessed April 19, 2021, https://www.blueletterbible.org/lang/lexicon/lexicon. cfm?Strongs=G2489&t=KJV.

7. Blue Letter Bible, s.v. *"magdalēnē,"* accessed April 19, 2021, https://www.blueletterbible.org/lang/lexicon/lexicon. cfm?Strongs=G3094&t=KJV.

8. Blue Letter Bible, s.v. *"migdāl,"* accessed April 20, 2021, https://www.blueletterbible.org/lang/lexicon/lexicon. cfm?t=kjv&strongs=h4026.

9. Thomas Timpson, *Memoirs of Mrs. Elizabeth Fry* (New York: Stanford and Swords, 1847), 31–32, https://archive.org/details/memoirsmrseliza01timpgoog/page/n3/mode/2up.

CHAPTER 9

1. Blue Letter Bible, s.v. *"brechō,"* accessed April 19, 2021, https://www.blueletterbible.org/lang/lexicon/lexicon. cfm?Strongs=G1026&t=KJV.

2. Blue Letter Bible, s.v. *"proskyneō,"* accessed April 19, 2021, https://www.blueletterbible.org/lang/lexicon/lexicon. cfm?Strongs=G4352&t=KJV.

3. Blue Letter Bible, s.v. *"kataphileō,"* accessed April 19, 2021, https://www.blueletterbible.org/lang/lexicon/lexicon. cfm?Strongs=G2705&t=KJV.

4. Fanny Crosby, "Blessed Assurance," Hymnal.net, accessed April 20, 2021, https://www.hymnal.net/en/hymn/h/308.

5. Fanny J. Crosby, *Fanny Crosby's Life-Story* (New York: Every Where Publishing, 1903), 160, https://archive.org/details/fannycrosbyslife00hers/page/160/mode/2up.

6. Fanny J. Crosby, *Fanny Crosby's Story of Ninety-Four Years*, retold by S. Trevena Jackson (New York: Fleming

H. Revell, 1915), 156, https://archive.org/details/
fannycrosbysstor00stre/page/156/mode/2up.

CHAPTER 10

1. Blue Letter Bible, s.v. *"praus,"* accessed April 19, 2021,
   https://www.blueletterbible.org/lang/lexicon/lexicon.
   cfm?Strongs=G4239&t=KJV.
2. Henry George Liddell and Robert Scott, *A Greek-English Lexicon*, s.v. *"πρᾶος,"* Tufts University, accessed April 20, 2021, http://www.perseus.tufts.edu/hopper/text?doc=Perseu s:text:1999.04.0057:entry=pra=os.
3. Xenophon, *On Horsemanship*, trans. H. G. Dakyns, Project Gutenberg, updated January 15, 2013, https://www. gutenberg.org/files/1176/1176-h/1176-h.htm.
4. Sarah H. Bradford, *Scenes in the Life of Harriet Tubman*, University of North Carolina, 2000, https://docsouth.unc. edu/neh/bradford/bradford.html.
5. Bradford, *Scenes in the Life of Harriet Tubman*.
6. Bradford, *Scenes in the Life of Harriet Tubman*.
7. Bradford, *Scenes in the Life of Harriet Tubman*.
8. Blue Letter Bible, s.v. *"'ûl,"* accessed April 19, 2021,
   https://www.blueletterbible.org/lang/Lexicon/lexicon.
   cfm?strongs=H193&t=KJV.
9. Blue Letter Bible, s.v. *"qāvâ,"* accessed April 19, 2021,
   https://www.blueletterbible.org/lang/lexicon/lexicon.
   cfm?Strongs=H6960&t=KJV.

CHAPTER 11

1. Blue Letter Bible, s.v. *"ḥēp̄eṣ,"* accessed April 19, 2021,
   https://www.blueletterbible.org/lang/lexicon/lexicon.
   cfm?Strongs=H2656&t=KJV.
2. Blue Letter Bible, s.v. *"kaleō,"* accessed April 19, 2021,
   https://www.blueletterbible.org/lang/lexicon/lexicon.
   cfm?Strongs=G2564&t=KJV.

3. Blue Letter Bible, s.v. "*klēsis*," accessed April 19, 2021, https://www.blueletterbible.org/lang/lexicon/lexicon.cfm?Strongs=G2821&t=KJV.

4. Joyce Meyer, *Knowing God Intimately* (New York: Warner Books, 2003), 54, 107, https://archive.org/details/knowinggodintima00meye/page/106/mode/2up.

5. Meyer, *Knowing God Intimately*, 19.

6. Meyer, *Knowing God Intimately*, 19.

7. Meyer, *Knowing God Intimately*, 133–134.

8. Meyer, *Knowing God Intimately*, 135.

Chapter 12

1. Blue Letter Bible, s.v. "*nikaō*," accessed April 19, 2021, https://www.blueletterbible.org/lang/lexicon/lexicon.cfm?Strongs=G3528&t=KJV.

2. Blue Letter Bible, s.v. "*hypernikaō*," accessed April 19, 2021, https://www.blueletterbible.org/lang/lexicon/lexicon.cfm?Strongs=G5245&t=KJV; Blue Letter Bible, s.v. "*hyper*," accessed April 19, 2021, https://www.blueletterbible.org/lang/lexicon/lexicon.cfm?strongs=G5228&t=KJV.

3. Blue Letter Bible, s.v. "*Ḥannâ*," accessed April 19, 2021, https://www.blueletterbible.org/lang/lexicon/lexicon.cfm?Strongs=H2584&t=KJV.

4. Blue Letter Bible, s.v. "*Šᵊmûʾēl*," accessed April 19, 2021, https://www.blueletterbible.org/lang/lexicon/lexicon.cfm?Strongs=H8050&t=KJV.

5. Lucinda Vardey, *Mother Teresa: A Simple Path* (New York: Random House, 1995), 185; Kent M. Keith, "The Mother Teresa Connection," Anyway: The Paradoxical Commandments, accessed April 20, 2021, https://www.paradoxicalcommandments.com/mother-teresa-connection/.

6. Andrea Morris, "Evangelist Beth Moore Says Scripture Helped Her Overcome Childhood Sexual Abuse," CBN News, March 1, 2020, https://www1.cbn.com/cbnnews/us/2020/march/evangelist-beth-moore-says-scripture-helped-her-overcome-childhood-sexual-abuse.

7. Beth Moore (@BethMooreLPM), "This culture's training us to be fragile," Twitter, December 4, 2019, 8:08 a.m., https://twitter.com/BethMooreLPM/status/1202212977241460741.

8. Beth Moore (@BethMooreLPM), "I did not surrender to a calling of man when I was 18 years old," Twitter, October 21, 2019, 9:24 a.m., https://twitter.com/BethMooreLPM/status/1186272022365638657.

CHAPTER 13

1. Blue Letter Bible, s.v. "ēzer," accessed April 19, 2021, https://www.blueletterbible.org/lang/lexicon/lexicon.cfm?Strongs=H5828&t=KJV.

2. Donald E. Gowan, ed., *The Westminster Theological Wordbook of the Bible* (Louisville, KY: Westminster John Knox Press, 2003), 312, https://www.google.com/books/edition/The_Westminster_Theological_Wordbook_of/obj6XCWIX1AC?hl=en&gbpv=1.

3. Blue Letter Bible, s.v. "ēzer."

4. Blue Letter Bible, s.v. "neḡed," accessed April 19, 2021, https://www.blueletterbible.org/lang/lexicon/lexicon.cfm?Strongs=H5048&t=KJV.

5. Barbara Hughes, *Disciplines of a Godly Woman* (Wheaton, IL: Crossway Books, 2001), 152, https://www.google.com/books/edition/Disciplines_of_a_Godly_Woman/nyS656Fg2YYC?hl=en&gbpv=0.

6. David Biale, "The God With Breasts: El Shaddai in the Bible," *History of Religions* 21, no. 3 (February 1982): 240–256, https://www.jstor.org/stable/1062160; Blue Letter Bible, s.v. "šad," accessed April 19, 2021, https://www.blueletterbible.org/lang/lexicon/lexicon.cfm?Strongs=H7699&t=KJV.

7. Blue Letter Bible, s.v. "skeuos," accessed April 19, 2021, https://www.blueletterbible.org/lang/lexicon/lexicon.cfm?Strongs=G4632&t=KJV.

8. Blue Letter Bible, s.v. *"asthenēs,"* accessed April 19, 2021, https://www.blueletterbible.org/lang/lexicon/lexicon.cfm?Strongs=G772&t=KJV.

9. Blue Letter Bible, s.v. *"timē,"* accessed April 19, 2021, https://www.blueletterbible.org/lang/lexicon/lexicon.cfm?Strongs=G5092&t=KJV.

10. "The Consequences of Fatherlessness," Fathers.com, accessed April 19, 2021, https://fathers.com/statistics-and-research/the-consequences-of-fatherlessness/.

CHAPTER 14

1. Leah MarieAnn Klett, "John MacArthur Clarifies Views on Beth Moore, Women Preachers: 'Empowering Women Makes Weak Men,'" Christian Post, November 13, 2019, https://www.christianpost.com/news/john-macarthur-clarifies-views-on-beth-moore-women-preachers-empowering-women-makes-weak-men.html.

2. Blue Letter Bible, "TR Concordance for λαλεῖν," accessed April 19, 2021, https://www.blueletterbible.org/lang/lexicon/inflections.cfm?strongs=G2980&t=KJV&ot=TR&word=%CE%BB%CE%B1%CE%BB%CE%B5%E1%BF%96%CE%BD; Blue Letter Bible, s.v. *"laleō,"* accessed April 19, 2021, https://www.blueletterbible.org/lang/lexicon/lexicon.cfm?strongs=G2980&t=KJV.

3. Blue Letter Bible, s.v. *"didaskō,"* accessed April 19, 2021, https://www.blueletterbible.org/lang/lexicon/lexicon.cfm?page=1&strongs=G1321&t=KJV#lexResults.

4. Blue Letter Bible, s.v. *"authenteō,"* accessed April 19, 2021, https://www.blueletterbible.org/lang/lexicon/lexicon.cfm?Strongs=G831&t=KJV.

5. *Merriam-Webster,* s.v. "usurp," accessed April 19, 2021, https://www.merriam-webster.com/dictionary/usurp.

6. Richard Clark Kroeger and Catherine Clark Kroeger, *I Suffer Not a Woman* (Grand Rapids, MI: Baker Books, 1992), 99, https://www.amazon.com/Suffer-Not-Woman-Rethinking-Evidence/dp/0801052505.

7. *Merriam-Webster*, s.v. "authentic," accessed April 19, 2021, https://www.merriam-webster.com/dictionary/authentic.

8. Stephan A. Hoeller, "The Genesis Factor," Gnosis Archive, September 1997, http://gnosis.org/genesis.html.

9. Kroeger and Kroeger, *I Suffer Not a Woman*, 103.

10. J. Lee Grady, *10 Lies the Church Tells Women* (Lake Mary, FL: Charisma House, 2006), 118, https://www.google.com/books/edition/10_Lies_the_Church_Tells_Women/CTN3kFm3CLMC?hl=en&gbpv=0.

11. Blue Letter Bible, s.v. "*hayil*," accessed April 19, 2021, https://www.blueletterbible.org/lang/lexicon/lexicon.cfm?page=5&strongs=H2428&t=KJV#lexResults.

12. For more on the chayil woman, see John Eckhardt, *Chayil* (Lake Mary, FL: Charisma House, 2019).

13. Blue Letter Bible, "Psalm 68:11: Interlinear," accessed April 19, 2021, https://www.blueletterbible.org/kjv/psa/68/1/t_conc_546011.

14. "Psalm 68:11," Bible Gateway, accessed April 19, 2021, https://www.biblegateway.com/verse/en/Psalm%2068%3A11. Note that the equivalent verse was checked in versions with differing versification.

CHAPTER 15

1. *Merriam-Webster*, s.v. "legacy," accessed April 19, 2021, https://www.merriam-webster.com/dictionary/legacy.

My Free
Gift to You

Dear Reader, I'm so happy you read my book. God is calling you to say yes to Him and the role He has created just for you. Your bold step of faith will create a legacy that lives on from generation to generation.

As a thank-you, I am offering you the e-book for *The Esther Anointing*...for free!

To get this FREE gift,
PLEASE GO TO
michellemcclainbooks.com/esther

— GOD BLESS, —

Michelle McClain-Walters